TEENS, PUT ON THE ARMOR OF GOD

A Teenager's Guide to a Relationship with God

JOHN GLOEGE

ISBN 979-8-89428-693-8 (paperback)
ISBN 979-8-89428-694-5 (digital)

Christian Faith Publishing
832 Park Avenue
Meadville, PA 16335
www.christianfaithpublishing.com

All scripture included is from the NIV Bible translation, unless otherwise noted.

Printed in the United States of America

To my seven wonderful grandchildren: Julia and Amy Zenzen, Robbie and Sydney Cole, Donovan Brown, and Marcus and Martez Manuel. They have all been an amazing blessing in my life.

To my elementary Sunday school teacher, Ellen Swanson. Ellen lovingly helped me and countless children, over many years in Glenwood, Minnesota, start to grow a relationship with God.

CONTENTS

I believe that building a strong relationship with God as early as possible will better help children put on the armor of God and recruit His protection. We need to foster a strong connection between our children and God to allow our youth to have greater opportunities for achievement and to set them up for a more successful life.

Jesus's love is not only for adults. On the contrary, Jesus says in Luke 18:16–17, "Let the little children come to me, and do not hinder them, for the kingdom of God belongs to such as these. Truly I tell you, anyone who will not receive the kingdom of God like a little child will never enter it." Jesus loved the children when here on His earthly pilgrimage. He wanted the youth to act the part of fun-loving and carefree children. Therefore, Jesus can relate to children and teenagers, so why shouldn't children and teens be able to relate to Him?

God wants us to have fun and experience all the great and beautiful things He has created for us in this world. Also, don't sell God's sense of humor short. I'm sure He finds humor in the way we move through our lives. God's sense of humor is beyond our comprehension. If the Lord who created us could laugh at us, we certainly should humble ourselves and laugh at ourselves.

I believe our culture, to some extent, promotes that it is of lesser importance for a child or teenager to have a strong relationship with the Lord than it is for an adult. Maybe it is because society feels the youth have more time as life transpires to establish a strong bond with the Lord than adults have. One of Satan's favorite tools is to deceive people into thinking they have all the time in the world to develop a relationship with God. Every day he can delay our spiritual growth is another day he can have a better chance to get his hooks into us.

Our society may have the belief that children and teens have less capability to comprehend the mysteries of God, and that the child can be educated about the Word of God at a later time. Also, society may indeed have the attitude that children are not yet important in the grand scheme of life and do not take seriously the importance of youth developing an early relationship with the Lord.

However, if Jesus has the viewpoint that unless we become as a child, we will not enter into eternal life, our culture should be encouraging youth to have a solid relationship with the Lord. We should be fostering a connection between our children and God. It is to the advantage of all for children to engage in a relationship with the Lord at as early an age as possible. Adults and society will benefit from children and teens having a good relationship with God because children and teens will likely get into less trouble because of the positive effect of being close to the Lord. Less trouble at school and with the law will allow greater opportunities for achievement and success at an early stage of life. An early bond with God will likely get the youth off to a good start in life and set him- or herself up for a fulfilling life.

Parents should also promote this connection between God and children in their family worship traditions and rituals. Some churches do a great job in their faith formation programs. Other churches would benefit today's youth by strengthening their youth groups, youth religious education, and other programs for youth. Strong leadership is vital to an effective church youth group.

One church I know of promotes the idea, "Kids are not the church of tomorrow. They are the church of today." I believe that is a very powerful slogan. A church is only as strong as the youth of that congregation. Parents, churches, and society must work at making it desirable for teens to pursue and develop a relationship with the Lord at as young of an age as feasible.

As in many things in life, the earlier things are taught and exposed to people, the easier it is for them to learn skills or concepts.

For example, a very young child more easily learns to swim compared to a thirty-year-old attempting to learn. The very young child has no fear of the water and no fear of failing to master the task. Skills such as learning to ride a bicycle and learning to golf are also examples of activities easier to learn at an early age. Therefore, indoctrinating a love of God at an early age may be easier for parents and youth working together.

Another reason it is important for children to establish a relationship with God at an early age is a seemingly prevalent attitude that it is not *cool* for kids to demonstrate a strong relationship with God in front of other kids. The power of peer pressure is extremely difficult for teenagers to contradict. Teenagers sometimes tend to develop a nonconforming attitude that feeds off peer pressure and the need to impress their peers. It is likely parents will have less success by waiting longer to start encouraging their children to connect with the Lord because of nonconformity and peer pressure. Laying a solid foundation as early as possible will better help children put on God's armor and resist negative peer pressure.

Connecting with other like-minded children relating to a loving relationship with the Lord develops a positive support system for teenagers. Peer support can be a very powerful influence. Being involved with a church youth group can be a great way for teens to develop their faith and strengthen their bond with the Lord. Youth groups offer great social networking with similar-aged kids. The social connection with peers that church youth groups afford can be invaluable. Nothing is more important to teenagers than peer acceptance.

From a teenager's standpoint, the best part of a good church youth group is the fun they have! In a well-organized youth group with strong and innovative leadership, the youth engage in many fun and exciting activities throughout the year. Field trips, attending a variety of events, and social functions are among the typical church youth group activities. There are also community-building projects that involve helping the less fortunate and also help develop an attitude of service. Character development occurs with peers in a fun way. What a wonderful way to help build a Christian foundation!

In a church I've attended, I am always amazed at the positive energy the youth groups display at the church services, especially when they have the opportunity to present their activities to the congregation. It is easy to see the genuine joy they portray in their presentations, photos, and enthusiasm at church.

ACKNOWLEDGMENTS

I would like to thank my daughter, Mary Zenzen, for her technical help in the writing of this book. Also, the insight from my friend and colleague Shannon Arens proved invaluable in delving into the mind of a teenager.

CHAPTER 1

Peer Acceptance and Peer Pressure

I had the privilege of teaching and coaching teenagers for thirty-three years in my career as a physical education teacher and coach in Princeton, Minnesota. Most of these years were spent working with middle-school-aged kids, grades six to eight. Middle school can be an awkward age in which kids are going through many physical and psychological changes. These changes can raise many questions in a teenager's mind. Middle school years are a very unique and sometimes unpredictable time in a person's life.

From many years of working with teenagers, particularly middle-school kids, I have developed an insight into the mind of this age-group. One thing I have learned is that nothing is more important to a teenager than being liked and approved of by their peers. Teens have a paramount need to be accepted by their peers. This need to fit in and be recognized by friends can cause a teenager to do things and act in ways that are not typical for him or her. Teenagers will even sometimes do things that will jeopardize their safety in order to conform to their peer group. Sometimes a teenager will risk getting into trouble with school authorities or even the law to gain the approval of their peers.

There is an almost unparalleled compulsion for teenagers to fit into a peer group. Teens are many times at a point in their lives that they are figuring out who they are and where they belong in life. Middle school and high school years are very formative years in a person's life. While going through the challenging, unpredictable, and sometimes confusing teenage years, it is vital for most kids to feel accepted by their peer group.

Peer acceptance can be defined as the degree a child is socially accepted or rejected by his or her peer group. In their struggle to be accepted by their peers in a positive way, teenagers encounter *peer pressure* along the way. Teens are sometimes faced with situations that force them to weigh the possible consequences of doing something that goes against their values, against the powerful desire to fit into their desired peer group. Peer pressure is defined as influence from one's peer group.

Peer pressure can be positive or negative, and it can be direct or indirect. An example of direct negative peer pressure would be peers asking a person to drink beer at an underage party. Direct peer pressure is peers directly asking someone to do something. Indirect negative peer pressure is what one sees and hears other teenagers doing. For example, a person seeing others wearing a certain style of clothing may influence the person to follow suit and wear the same style of clothes in order to fit in. It is an unspoken peer pressure.

There are times when peer pressure can be positive as well. An example of direct positive peer pressure is classmates encouraging someone to study hard for an upcoming exam in order to meet a class goal, which would result in a class reward. An example of indirect positive peer pressure would be a male athlete dressed in jeans and a tee shirt observing most of his peers dressed in a suit coat and tie for a team athletic banquet. The athlete would be more likely to wear a suit coat and tie at the next similar event in order to fit in better with his teammates. Again, the indirect pressure, whether negative or positive, is unspoken.

In many situations, the pressure a person feels is self-imposed. Especially in the case of teenagers, the event is magnified in the mind to create a crisis situation. Teenagers have less life experience in dealing with situations in which they are in a minority and, in their strong desire to fit in, can feel almost panic-stricken to fit in with others. The event and the perceived possible consequences of not conforming can be blown out of proportion in the teenager's mind. Therefore, sometimes it is the pressure a person is putting upon themselves that escalates the situation into something bigger than it actually is.

Even though peer pressure is sometimes self-imposed, it is a very real and powerful presence in the lives of teenagers. The compelling need to feel connected with one's desired peer group can influence teens to do many questionable things to satisfy and amuse their peers.

CHAPTER 2

Dealing with Peer Pressure

One of the most common topics in regard to teenagers, in which the term *peer pressure* is associated with, is drug use. Experimentation with alcohol, tobacco, marijuana, and other even more dangerous drugs is often at the center of peer pressure for teens. Often the pressure to partake involves not only using alcohol or other drugs but also the encouragement by others to overindulge in the drugs. The excessive use of a drug or drugs obviously presents many serious dangers and possible tragic outcomes.

A 2015 report from the Centers for Disease Control and Prevention revealed that more than 2,200 people die from alcohol poisoning each year in the United States. Alcohol poisoning deaths are caused by drinking a large amount of alcohol in a short period of time. This can result in very high levels of alcohol in the body, which can shut down critical areas of the brain that control breathing, heart rate, and body temperature, resulting in death.

The need to fit in and be accepted by peers can cause people, particularly teenagers, to engage in behaviors that go against their better judgment. In the case of overindulgence in alcohol, initiations into groups of peers can be a culprit. For newly independent college students, the freedom of being on their own can cause teenagers to stretch their boundaries and remove the guard rails that were present while living at home. Younger teens may combine the forces of peer pressure with a feeling of rebellion against parents and/or authority as reasons to succumb to excessive use of alcohol or other drugs.

Peer pressure has been around for as long as mankind has been in existence. The need to belong and be accepted is human nature. Since around the early 1960s, teenage drug use (in addition to alcohol) has been a societal concern. Many of these peer pressure situations occur at unsupervised parties in which kids gather. Schools have been forced to address the issue of teenage drug use as behaviors have changed, priorities have shifted, and even motivation to strive for goals has suffered among many teenage students who use drugs.

Schools offer many programs to educate students about drugs and how to deal with the peer pressure teenagers will likely encounter. The school programs attempt to equip teens with the skills to resist direct and indirect forms of peer pressure by offering techniques to *say no* and other strategies to avoid giving in to the pressure. The methods taught are designed to help the teens turn down peer pressure gracefully, and the techniques aim at not *burning bridges* with their peers.

Another strategy programs use is teaching teenagers to prepare in advance for specific peer pressure situations they may be faced with. The idea is to anticipate situations where conditions may be present for peer pressure to manifest itself and to have a plan ready to deal with the pressure. Many of the programs promote group discussion among classmates to express feelings about experiences they may have encountered in their young lives concerning peer pressure, what strategies may have been effective in dealing with peer pressure, being accepted by peers, and the consequences of saying no, as well as the fallout from going along with the crowd.

It is natural to want to fit in with others. Most people want to conform to the opinions and behaviors of the people they associate with. It is common for people to suppress their opinions when they sense their views are in the extreme minority. People often don't want to compromise their position in their peer group by *rocking the boat*. It is common for people to feel satisfied with the status quo and feel comfortable with their position of acceptance within the group. People, many times, just avoid taking the risk of being contrary.

Fear of other people's opinions is something that inhibits many people but particularly teenagers. There is a natural tendency for teenagers to be very mindful of the opinions of others. Because of their youth and limited life experience, teens usually have not fully established their identity. They are still finding where they fit in life. Teenagers' concerns about the views of others can dictate and alter their behaviors as they search for their place in society and in their peer group.

There is actually a word, *allodoxaphobia*, defined as the fear of hearing other people's opinions. The acronym FOPO, fear of other people's opinions, is used to describe this phobia. The fear of other people's opinions is a big part of what causes peer pressure. The path of least resistance is often to go along with the group and not express a contrary opinion. It is often easier and more comfortable to keep quiet and conform.

A young person can be greatly assisted by leaning on a healthy relationship with God when battling peer pressure. There are countless ways God can advocate for teenagers, and all of us, if we know Him. As Romans 8:31 states, "What then, shall we say in response to these things? If God is with us, who can be against us?"

CHAPTER 3

Self-Esteem

From my many years of teaching and coaching, I have learned how important healthy self-esteem is to teenagers. As I got to know certain kids better, I could get a sense of how they viewed themselves. I learned that the teenagers who were more confident in themselves had a higher success rate. There is a concept often expressed, "Whether you think you can or think you can't, you are right."

When confronting issues, a person who believes they can deal successfully with the situation is much more likely to effectively confront the dilemma compared to a person who doesn't feel confident in handling the situation. Children and all people who feel good about themselves, usually achieve more, are generally well-liked, and are more self-assured in their decision-making. Teenagers with healthy self-esteem, in many cases, are not afraid to strive for goals. One attribute builds on another, and the teen more quickly evolves into a productive person as opposed to a person with low self-esteem.

A teenager with strong self-esteem has a tremendous advantage when it comes to making responsible decisions and resisting peer pressure. A confident teen can more easily fight off negative influences because of the knowledge that if they are temporarily rejected by a peer group because of doing what is right, the self-assured teenager will land on their feet. They don't depend on the reinforcement of a peer group as much as a teen with lower self-esteem. The teenager with a healthy self-esteem can more easily stand up for their beliefs.

The terms *self-esteem* and *self-image* are often used interchangeably. The terms are very closely related. Self-esteem can be described as how you value yourself and the kind of person you think you are. Self-image is how you *see* yourself. Importantly, it also includes how you believe others see you. After reading the descriptions of these two terms, it is easy to understand why they are so important to people, particularly teenagers, as they learn who they are and how they fit into society.

When it comes right down to it, there may not be any attribute a person can have that is more important than healthy self-esteem. If a person values himself/herself in a positive way, the person tends to feel free to try new, challenging things as opposed to a person with low self-esteem. Because of self-confidence, a person with healthy self-esteem is usually more willing to risk failure and use trial and error to come up with solutions to situations. A confident person usually has the ability to bounce back from disappointment or failure.

One axiom I have heard throughout my life is "You must love yourself before you can love others." I believe this statement is very true, and I have learned and observed the principle in action in certain situations in my life. A person with self-esteem issues, many times, doesn't believe they are worthy to be loved.

Also, a person who doesn't feel good about himself or herself often finds something missing in themselves and may rely on others to fill that gap. This reliance can be very draining on the person trying to fill the void of the needy one. People who don't love themselves often don't understand why other people love them.

The person with low self-esteem sometimes puts a wall up in a relationship because they fear others will end the relationship with them. A person with low self-esteem may not want to risk *putting himself or herself out there* in a relationship for fear of rejection. I'm not referring exclusively to a romantic relationship. The relationship could be friendship, parent with child, teacher/coach with student, or any relationship where there is interaction.

Because of the extreme importance of healthy self-esteem in teenagers' lives, I always made attempting to make students feel good about themselves my number one priority in my years as an educator.

All but six of my thirty-three years were spent at the middle school level. It is at that age that I believe the matter of self-esteem is especially crucial. Middle school-aged kids can be very fragile concerning others' feelings about them. Mood swings in middle school years are extremely common and can even change throughout the course of a day. I tried to compliment and validate students whenever I saw the opportunity to do so.

Comparison can be evil when it comes to the erosion of self-esteem. We live in a society in which comparing ourselves to others is very common and natural. We tend to measure ourselves in relation to others, which can be a very slippery slope. Television and other media advertisements can offer an unrealistic view of what normal is. The actors in advertisements are usually *beautiful people* and can cause typical teenagers to question themselves when they compare themselves with the actors.

Comparing ourselves with others can cause us to try to become who we weren't meant to be. Instead of becoming obsessed with what is going on in others' lives, we should strive to attain the goals that fit best for our lives and to what we aspire to. As the saying goes, "We should run our own race."

The society in which we live is very competitive, and there can be pressure to match the success that others achieve. Comparing our accomplishments or lack of accomplishments with others can cause us to feel inferior if we dwell on how we measure up. Theodore Roosevelt is credited with the quote, "Comparison is the thief of joy." Alarmingly, *Psychology Today* revealed in January 2023 from its research that more than 10 percent of daily thoughts involved making a comparison of some kind.

It is important to remember that we are all created with different gifts, skill sets, and interests. Teenagers should strive to learn what their strengths, weaknesses, and interests are so they can pursue avenues in life appropriate for them. Learning and understanding who we are is one of life's great challenges. Being aware of our strengths and weaknesses is a big key in life. When we are honest and accurate in assessing ourselves, we are in a much better position to make career and life goals and determine a path to pursue those goals.

Teenagers and all of us must avoid trying to emulate people we admire if their path in life doesn't fit our strengths and interests. We must carve out our own path and be who we are meant to be. Comparing ourselves to others and obsessively envying them is not wise and usually counterproductive. We are all perfectly created according to God's plan for us. Scripture backs this up by saying in Psalm 139:13–14, "For you created my inmost being; you knit me together in my mother's womb. I praise you because I am fearfully and wonderfully made; your works are wonderful, I know that full well."

Fear can be another roadblock to a healthy self-esteem. It is difficult to feel good about ourselves when we are experiencing fear. Fear can paralyze us and prevent us from striving to fulfill the destiny God has for us. We must recognize when fear is holding us back and be courageous in overcoming the hold fear can have on us.

Earlier, I discussed FOPO, the fear of other people's opinions; and without a strong self-esteem, FOPO can definitely hold us back. We must have the confidence in ourselves to work through worrying about what others think. At some point in our lives, we must develop a sense of independence and be our own person.

Another area where fear can attack us is the fear of failure. We must develop a sense of resiliency and keep getting back up when we get knocked down. As the saying goes concerning failure, "All that matters is that we get back up one more time than we get knocked down."

I have learned in the course of my lifetime that one of the common denominators successful people have is mental toughness. Mental toughness is a personality trait that determines your ability to perform consistently under stress and pressure. Successful people have the ability to keep striving for their goals (persistence) and to overcome failure, not letting failure define them. Mental toughness separates people. Many will give up when the going gets tough, but as the saying goes, "When the going gets tough, the tough gets going."

CHAPTER 4

Self-Affirmation

After going through the importance of self-esteem and self-image as discussed in chapter 3, the question must be asked, "What can we do to strengthen our self-esteem?" This is a very tricky question because our self-esteem is largely based on previous experiences in our lives. We can't change the outcomes of past events in our lives. If our life experiences early in life yield positive results, we are more likely to have a more optimistic view of ourselves. Conversely, if our early life memories and experiences reflect unhappy circumstances, the way we feel about ourselves may have a more negative tint.

However, we can work at improving our self-esteem. In my book *Your Reward Shall Not Come of This Earth*, I wrote in the epilogue about the value of self-affirmation in a person's life. We can define self-affirmation as the act of affirming one's own worthiness and value as an individual for beneficial effect. This definition fits perfectly with self-esteem since self-esteem is based on how we value ourselves. The reason self-affirmation is so important in our lives is that it gives us the power to change negative thinking patterns and replace them with positive ones. There is not much in life more valuable than thinking positively, especially when it comes to how we feel about ourselves.

As I grow older, life has taught me that life can be a self-fulfilling prophecy to a large degree. It goes back to what I mentioned earlier in the book, "Whether you think you can or think you can't, you are right." The mindset we have concerning issues and situations we encounter in life goes a long way in determining the outcome of the circumstance. Our attitude can help us achieve success in life situations by thinking positively about the impending results. The way we think about ourselves, in large part, determines our confidence level and how successful we will be in life.

An affirmation is usually a sentence of powerful words put together in a positive statement. This statement is aimed to tap into the conscious and unconscious mind to motivate you to reach your full potential in life. Affirmation is self-talk and is aimed at convincing oneself of something. Self-affirmation can be used in any area of one's life and is, in a way, *brainwashing* oneself in a positive fashion. Affirmations often start with the words *I am* and are usually in the present tense.

Concerning self-affirmation relating to improving self-esteem, the affirmations should be centered on improving how a person views his/her worth. Some examples of self-affirmations to help bolster self-esteem are the following:

1. I am worthy, and I deserve everything I want in life.
2. I love myself unconditionally
3. I am competent, smart, and able.
4. I am growing and changing for the better.
5. I love the person I am becoming.
6. Every day I am becoming a better version of myself.

For teenagers, self-affirmations can be used for many situations in school. For example, in preparing for a test, the student may declare readiness by affirming, "I am confident and prepared going into this test." Another affirmation would be, "I will do well on this test because I have studied the content we will be tested on."

In preparation for a competition in a school activity, one might affirm, "I am confident in my ability to be successful in this upcoming competition." Another affirmation would be, "I am improving every day in this activity, and I know I will succeed due to my preparation."

An example of self-affirming a teenager's strength and resolve when the possibility of encountering negative peer pressure exists would be, "I am strong and can make the right decision if offered an alcoholic beverage at the party." Another affirmation states, "I can handle the rejection of my peers if they don't respect my decision not to drink alcohol."

I have used self-affirmation in a very close relationship with prayer. The affirmations listed above can be a form of prayer by adding the words, "Lord, thank You that...," in front of each self-affirmation. Remember, we should pray as though the prayer request has already been granted.

Self-affirmations are phrases you can say either aloud or in your head. To be most effective, the affirmations should be repeated at least three times a day. More than one affirmation can be recited per session.

Importantly, self-affirmation can help us grow as Christians, affirming that we are growing closer to the Lord each day. "Prayer is becoming a larger part of my life," "I am bold in the Lord and take advantage of opportunities to spread His word," and "I look forward to reading the Bible and meditating on His word" are all examples of self-affirmations to help us grow in our faith.

Philippians 4:13 is what I call the father of all self-affirmations. It says, "I can do all this through Him who gives me strength." This affirmation covers it all. All other affirmations are born from Philippians 4:13 and are specific affirmations for particular desires of the heart of the petitioner.

Self-affirmations can yield life-changing results for people who use them sincerely and diligently. A person has to be serious in his/her desire for improvement in a particular area of life for the affirmations to be effective. According to deepstash.com, to get the most benefit from affirmations, you'll want to start a regular practice and make it a habit. You can start affirmation sessions that last about three to five minutes and build in time from there. Affirmations should be recited at least twice a day. Stating affirmations upon waking up and getting into bed are often effective times. Each affirmation should be repeated about ten times.

I have used self-affirmation for various things in my life, and I have found them to be extremely effective. In a way, the practice of self-affirmation confirms the idea of *mind over matter* that we hear so often. I think everyone can think of situations in their lives where they have *willed* something to happen through an intense desire strengthened by the mind. There is so much untapped potential in the power of what the mind can do for us. Affirmations are a great way to tap into what the mind can do to benefit us.

CHAPTER 5

What Is Spiritual Warfare?

One vital reason to have an early relationship with God is to combat spiritual warfare. Spiritual warfare can be defined as the act of fighting against Satan when he tries to keep us from God's calling. Ephesians 6:11 tells us, "Put on the full armor of God, so that you can take your stand against the devil's schemes." What is the armor of God? A soldier's tools include a belt, breastplate, shoes, shield, helmet, and sword. In comparison, a Christian's armor of God consists of truth, righteousness, the Gospel, faith, salvation, the Word of God, and prayer. A soldier's equipment is designed for their earthly combat while a Christian's protection is geared for spiritual warfare.

Ephesians 6:14–15 tells us, "Stand firm then, with the belt of truth buckled around your waist, with the breastplate of righteousness in place, and with your feet fitted with the readiness that comes from the gospel of peace." The belt of truth represents our integrity, which is the quality of being honest and having strong moral principles that you refuse to change. The armor of God for all of us starts with knowing the truth and being loyal to the truth. The foundation of faith is truth, and without faith, it is impossible to please God.

Hebrews 11:6 says, "And without faith it is impossible to please God, because anyone who comes to him must believe that he exists and that he rewards those who earnestly seek him." The truth is our fundamental defense against spiritual warfare. The belt of truth gives us the stability to counteract evil like a weightlifter's belt protects his or her core when under the stress of lifting.

The breastplate of righteousness goes around our upper body and gives us protection for our vital organs. The breastplate of righteousness represents the purity of the heart. Our motives must be clean, and our conscience should bother us when we do not live up to God's expectations. The importance of a pure heart is emphasized in Psalm 24:3–4 when it says, "Who may ascend the mountain of the Lord? Who may stand in his holy place? The one who has clean hands and a pure heart, who does not trust in an idol or swear by a false god."

Ephesians 6:15 tells us that our feet are to be fitted with the readiness that comes from the gospel of peace. Soldiers wore cleats on their shoes, similar to football cleats, in order to provide steady footing. These cleated shoes gave soldiers a solid foundation from the ground up and helped keep them from slipping. Believers are given the gospel of peace in order to be ready for battle and to help others facing spiritual attacks. The gospel of peace leads us to living a life of serenity. When we have peace and serenity, we are showing God we trust Him.

Finally, Ephesians 6:16–17 instructs us, "In addition to all this, take up the shield of faith, with which you can extinguish all the flaming arrows of the evil one. Take the helmet of salvation and the sword of the Spirit, which is the word of God." The word of God is above any weapon this world can present. Hebrews 4:12 describes it this way, "For the word of God is alive and active. Sharper than any double-edged sword, it penetrates even to dividing soul and spirit, joints and marrow; it judges the thoughts and attitudes of the heart."

With all of the spiritual warfare going on in society today and the enemy busy at work, it is essential for us all to be fully dressed in God's armor. We need God to be at our side as we encounter the spiritual warfare existing in the world every day. We need God to help us, through the Holy Spirit, to recognize evil, resist temptation, and discern what is right from wrong from the viewpoint of God.

Spiritual warfare can also be described as a *battle for souls*. Spiritual warfare is very real and seems stronger than ever in today's society. One needs only to flip through the television channels, looking at the content present for people of all ages to view. Children, if not properly supervised, are exposed to an abundance of material they should not be viewing or hearing. Even commercial advertisements, in many cases, are not suitable for young eyes, ears, and minds to absorb. Sexual inferences in advertisements are extremely common and seem to have been accepted as normal in our society.

Satan seems busier with each passing year as he relishes in society's increasingly permissive values. It seems as though the pattern of society's morals loosening will only continue. The only thing that will reverse this trend would be a major shift in society's values. It seems very unlikely that the morals of society will get stronger before they get weaker.

The first step in effectively engaging in spiritual warfare is to recognize it exists. We can't be in denial that spiritual warfare is a real thing and is all around us. Another way to describe spiritual warfare is like being in a wrestling match with persons without bodies. We could call spiritual warfare *the invisible battle*. It is hard to fight against something we can't physically see or touch.

It is easy to see why God's armor is so important for us in our struggle against evil. Ephesians 6:12 says it this way, "For our struggle is not against flesh and blood, but against the rulers, against the authorities, against the powers of this dark world and against the spiritual forces of evil in the heavenly realms."

Fortunately for us, Jesus lives in our souls as the Holy Spirit. Jesus will win any battle He is faced with. However, we need to employ His powers, which provide strength, wisdom, and discernment. Without a relationship with God, we are at a massive disadvantage. We must be fully dressed in God's armor and learn to lean on Him in times of crisis.

We must remember that God has given us the power to rebuke Satan when we feel his presence in the midst. Luke 10:19 tells us, "Behold, I have given you authority to tread on serpents and scorpions, and over all the power of the enemy, and nothing shall hurt you." Many believers are afraid of the devil and the evil of darkness. However, the truth is they are already defeated, and in Jesus's name, we have been given authority over them. How do we rebuke Satan and demons? It can be as easy as saying, "Satan, I rebuke you in the name of Jesus! You have no power over me. I am a child of God."

It is easy to realize the importance of parents' upbringing from an early age. The earlier parents can help establish a Christian foundation and a love of God in their children, the easier it will be for the children to effectively recognize spiritual warfare and deal with it appropriately. Battling with evil in the world without a foundation based on God is like going into war without any defense or protection.

CHAPTER 6

The Power of Prayer

One of the most important and effective way to put on God's armor to battle spiritual warfare is through prayer. Prayer is the weapon that can defend us against any warfare or forces that can come up against us. Prayer is a major component of the Christian faith. Not only will prayer help us in the area of spiritual warfare but in all areas of our lives. Prayer is our vehicle of communication with the Lord. Prayer should be used for our protection, our desires, the glorification of God, and as an expression of gratitude for our blessings.

In my opinion, some people get *stuck* or intimidated concerning the subject of prayer through a perceived lack of understanding about it. Some feel they don't know how to pray, feeling there is an exact format that needs to be followed. Others question whether their prayers are heard, becoming impatient when prayers are not answered in a timely fashion. Bad things happening in the lives of people also create doubts as to the effectiveness of prayer for some.

It can be difficult for some people to engage in what they perceive as one-way communication. It is hard for some not to hear immediately from the Lord after prayer. We must learn to pray persistently to God for things we earnestly desire. Persistent prayer is the prayer that doesn't give up. It's praying for something until God either answers our prayer, or He tells us to stop praying for that particular request. Persistent prayer is standing in faith that God will answer your prayer.

Ephesians 6:18 says about persistent prayer, "And pray in the Spirit on all occasions with all kinds of prayers and requests. With this in mind, be alert and always keep on praying for all the Lord's people." In addition, James 5:16 declares, "Therefore confess your sins to each other and pray for each other so that you may be healed." The prayer of a righteous person is powerful and effective.

I believe that prayer sometimes stalls because of a lack of faith that prayers are *getting through* to God. Because we usually don't hear the audible voice of God respond back to us during prayer, it can be easy to become discouraged concerning prayer. We need to have faith, pray persistently, and be patient on the subject of prayer.

To help deal with impatience and doubt that can occur as a result of not hearing the audible response from God to our prayers, we need to learn how to listen for God's unspoken, sometimes subtle, reply to our prayers. After we pray, we need to reflect, meditate, and listen for the way God responds to our prayers. We have to give God time to answer on His timetable and need to be observant in our search for His answers. For us to be patient in listening for God's response to our prayer, it often requires us to spend quiet time alone after we pray. We need to give God time to express His response to us. We can't give God a timeline to follow. Listening to that *still and small voice of God* is invaluable in recognizing God's answers to our prayers.

As Dr. Robert Jeffers has said, "Prayer is not about bending God's will to our will, but rather about bending our will to conform to His." We must pray persistently and boldly for what we desire but must accept what God determines. God ultimately knows what is best for us.

As to how to pray, prayer can be thought of as simply talking with the Lord. There is no set formula needed to communicate with God. It is just expressing what comes into our minds. The Lord already knows what we are thinking before we even express it to Him, so it shouldn't be threatening to us to talk with Him. In the Bible, the Lord does give us a format that we can use to pray when one of His disciples asks Him how to pray. Luke 11:1–4, describes the scene this way, "One day Jesus was praying in a certain place. When He finished, one of His disciples said to Him, 'Lord, teach us to pray, just as John taught his disciples.'" At that point, Jesus revealed the Lord's Prayer to the disciples.

The Lord's Prayer is simply an example of the way a prayer can be constructed and communicated. Jesus encourages us to pray often and ask for anything. Luke 11:9–10 says, "So I say to you: Ask and it will be given to you; seek and you will find; knock and the door will be opened to you. For everyone who asks receives; the one who seeks finds; and to the one who knocks, the door will be opened."

Teenagers would be wise and blessed to make Jesus their best friend. That friendship will serve as protective armor for all of life's challenges. Talk to Him any time as you would talk to a friend. This communication will be heard by Jesus as prayer. Jesus has many names because He is all things. Among some of the names of Jesus are the following: Wonderful, Counselor, Savior, Redeemer, Messiah, Teacher, and the Way, the Truth, and the Life. These are just a few of the many names used to define and describe Jesus. Can you possibly think of a better friend to have?

Prayer is the avenue to ask Jesus to advocate for us in all areas of life. We should ask for help in significant areas of life while at the same time recognizing that nothing is too small to pray for. We are not inconveniencing God by asking Him for what seems to be small in our eyes. He is all-knowing and can handle all things at the same time. We should ask God for all things we desire in life and trust Him to give us what is best for us.

I have learned and observed that prayer works. Many miraculous things have been accomplished because of prayer. God hears our every prayer and encourages us to come to Him in prayer. People with little faith may frame miracles as coincidences or luck, but people with faith in the Lord can easily make the connection of prayer leading to explosive blessings and miracles. We can have as close of a relationship with God as we desire. The intimacy of our relationship with God all depends on the time and effort we put into that relationship.

CHAPTER 7

Read and Study the Word of God

The most important investment we can make in this life is to study the Word of God. All the money we earn in life and all the earthly possessions we acquire during our lives will be meaningless when we die. As the saying goes, "When was the last time you ever saw a U-Haul behind a hearse?" We can't take it with us, and we must realize that when we take our last breath on earth, the only thing that matters is our relationship with God.

If we are wise, we must learn that we must live for the eternal, not the temporal. We must keep our *eye on the prize*. That prize, of course, is to live in heaven with the Lord for all of eternity. Nothing can compare with that prize, which is a gift freely given to us through Christ's death and resurrection for the forgiveness of all our sins. All we need to do to accept that gift is to confess our sins and receive Jesus into our hearts as our personal savior.

Therefore, we need to be well-versed in the Word of the Lord. It is important for us to read and research God's message to us in the Bible. I mentioned the importance of listening to God's response to our prayers. The Bible is God's inspired word communicated to us. The more we can understand the Word of God through the Bible, the more effectively we will understand and identify God's answers to our prayers. All the time we invest in studying God's Word is well spent because it helps us grow closer to Him.

It may sound difficult or intimidating to study God's Word in the Bible, but in reality, it is like so many things in life. The hardest part of the mission is just getting started. Once a person starts the process, it becomes less daunting to get into the Word on a regular basis. If we can make reading and studying the Bible a habit and a way of life, we begin to look forward to our sessions with the Lord and gain a better insight to the Word of God.

So what is the best way to study the Word of God? The best and most obvious method is to read the Bible. Again, reading the entire Bible sounds like a monumental task, but once started, the process becomes very achievable. Some people choose to read the Bible from front to back. Many others will start with the New Testament, leaving the Old Testament for last. Still, others will choose specific chapters to read in a random order. There is no wrong way to read the Bible.

Some people choose to read the New Testament first, even though it appears in the Bible after the Old Testament because it focuses on the life and teachings of Jesus and the Christian church. For many, reading the New Testament may be easier to understand and identify with. The New Testament may more closely resemble life as we know it today, compared with the Old Testament. Jesus gives us direct instruction concerning how we are to think and behave in life. Jesus often teaches through parables in the gospels, particularly Matthew, Mark, and Luke. A parable is a usually short, fictitious story that illustrates moral or spiritual lessons. The parable of the prodigal son is one example of a parable Jesus tells in the Bible.

The Old Testament explains the history of the creation of the world, the exodus of the Israelites, and the Ten Commandments given to Moses by God. The foundation for biblical prophecy is laid out in the Old Testament. Many promises that God will yet fulfill for the Jewish nation are contained in the Old Testament.

The book of Proverbs, found in the Old Testament, is an excellent teacher of life skills. Proverbs is a collection of wisdom from generations of godly people and reads like a "how to live your life" manual. There is so much wisdom to be gained from reading the book of Proverbs. It is outstanding teaching for all of us, and in particular, teenagers.

The book of Proverbs invites us to live with wisdom and in fear of the Lord. One of the most powerful and popular verses of the book is Proverbs 9:10, which says, "The fear of the Lord is the beginning of wisdom, and knowledge of the Holy One is understanding." I will discuss the book of Proverbs in more detail in chapter 16.

There is no substitution in life for studying the Bible. Getting into the Word of God will help us establish a strong relationship with the Lord and help us live for the eternal, rather than the temporary things this world has to offer.

CHAPTER 8

The Trinity and the Holy Spirit

The Bible teaches that the Father is God, that Jesus is God, and that the Holy Spirit is God. This is the Triune God that is described as the Holy Trinity. The Trinity is three coexistent, coeternal persons who are one God. It is vital to understand that the Trinity is not in any way suggesting there are three gods. It is one God with three different components. With that being said, each member of the Trinity is God. It is God in three persons. The Father, Son, and Holy Spirit are not parts of God; rather, each of them is God. The "God in three persons" Trinity is the reason I have used the names God and Jesus interchangeably in this book. I have also used the name Lord to describe God.

One of the most pertinent Bible verses addressing the Holy Trinity is Matthew 28:19, which says, "Therefore go and make disciples of all nations, baptizing them in the name of the Father and of the Son and of the Holy Spirit." In the act of baptism, the path to salvation of every sinner (all of us) is enabled by all three persons of the Trinity.

The concept of the Trinity is very difficult to comprehend. An infinite God cannot be fully described by a finite illustration or explanation. The Trinity is one of the mysteries that are hidden in God, which can never be known unless they are revealed by God. On one hand, the Trinity says that there are three distinct persons—Father, Son, and Holy Spirit—and that each of these persons is *God*. On the other hand, it says that there is one and only one God. Therefore, there is the appearance of a contradiction.

The good news is that, along with being incapable to fully understand the Trinity, we don't have to understand it completely. We are not expected to fully comprehend the Holy Trinity. Each entity of the Trinity has a major purpose. What we need to understand about the Trinity are the following three points:

1. God created the world.
2. God redeemed the world from sin through Jesus.
3. God is always present in the world guiding believers through the Holy Spirit.

Of the three entities of the Holy Trinity, God the Holy Spirit may be the most mysterious. In our prayers, we may not specifically mention the Holy Spirit as much as we do God the Father and Jesus. One of the chief roles of the Holy Spirit is to help Christians understand the idea that God is always present in the world and always with them.

Another main duty of the Holy Spirit is to elevate the name of Jesus Christ and help us understand the magnitude of the sacrifice He made on the cross for the remission of sins. The Holy Spirit forms the image of Christ in us. When we develop Christ-like character, it is the work of the Holy Spirit shaping us.

The Holy Spirit also bears witness to the heavenly Father and Jesus Christ and, one might say, does much behind the scenes to help us live a more godly life. We must be vigilant and open to the influence of the Holy Spirit. We can be guided in our decisions and be protected from physical and spiritual danger by listening to the Holy Spirit. Also known as the Comforter, the Holy Spirit can calm our fears and fill us with hope.

We must learn to follow the principles of the Holy Spirit and be tuned in to His voice to be led to live a life most pleasing to God. Through the power of the Holy Spirit, we are sanctified as we make our way through life. Sanctification is the process of changing us to be more like Jesus.

The voice of the Holy Spirit is described in the scriptures as still and small and of perfect mildness. The voice is like a whisper, but it can pierce even the soul and cause the heart to burn. Preachers like to refer to listening to that *still, small voice* instructing us to do what is right. That voice is the Holy Spirit talking to us. It is not a loud nor harsh voice and not a voice of thunder. The Holy Spirit is a subtle voice, gently trying to persuade us to do what is pleasing to the Lord. When we obey the Holy Spirit's instruction, we are on our way to living a Christian life.

Often the Holy Spirit will speak to us in our minds by giving us a thought or an idea. Sometimes the Holy Spirit will direct us by making an impression upon our hearts to do something, think something, or say something in alignment to God's will.

The doctrine of biblical inspiration, based on Christian theology, states that "God Himself breathed upon the human authors and editors. Through the influence of the Holy Spirit, His words were conveyed to His people." The human authors and editors were instruments or mediums through which God transmitted His message to the people.

The importance and reverence of the Holy Spirit are emphasized in Matthew 12:31–32 when it says, "And so I tell you, every kind of sin and slander can be forgiven, but blasphemy against the Spirit will not be forgiven. Anyone who speaks a word against the Son of Man will be forgiven, but anyone who speaks against the Holy Spirit will not be forgiven, either in this age or in the age to come."

Speaking against the Holy Spirit is known as the only unpardonable sin. It is interesting and alarming that speaking against Jesus will be forgiven, but speaking against the Holy Spirit is unforgivable.

The gifts of the Holy Spirit are described in 1 Corinthians 12, and the gifts are listed in verses 8–10. The noted gifts are wisdom, knowledge, faith, gifts of healing, working of miracles, prophecy, discerning of spirits, tongues, and interpretation of tongues.

Every person does not receive all of these gifts. First Corinthians 12:11 says, "All these are the work of one and the same Spirit, and he distributes them to each one, just as He determines." However,

1 Corinthians 12:7 indicates every person will receive at least one spiritual gift when it says, "Now to each one the manifestation of the Spirit is given for the common good." The Holy Spirit bestows upon all of us the gifts He wants us to possess for the glorification of God. Some are granted more spiritual gifts than others. It is important we discover our spiritual gifts and use them for the glorification of God.

One of the more interesting and mysterious gifts of the Holy Spirit is the gift of speaking in tongues. A baptized person who has accepted Christ as Savior could receive the gift of speaking in tongues from God and the Holy Spirit. This gift allows a person to speak in a language they otherwise have no knowledge of. Speaking in tongues may occur when a person makes incomprehensible sounds they believe are a language spoken through them by God. These instances of speaking in tongues often happen when a person is experiencing religious ecstasy or a trance.

Evidence of speaking in tongues is referenced in the Bible in Acts 2:4. The verse reveals, "All of them were filled with the Holy Spirit and began to speak in other tongues as the Spirit enabled them."

Many names and titles are used to describe the Holy Spirit. A few of the more common ones are Helper, Comforter, Counselor, Spirit of Truth, and Advocate. Note that all of these descriptors work to make our lives easier and assist us in good decision-making.

Jesus is responsible for some of the names used to describe the Holy Spirit. Jesus calls the Holy Spirit "Helper" when He says in John 14:16–17 (ESV), "And I will ask the Father, and He will give you another Helper, to be with you forever, even the Spirit of Truth, whom the world cannot receive, because it neither sees Him nor knows Him. You know Him, for He dwells with you and will be in you." In John 15:26, Jesus refers to the Holy Spirit as the Advocate by saying, "When the Advocate comes, whom I will send to you from the Father—the Spirit of truth who goes out from the Father-He will testify about me."

You may have heard the title Holy Ghost and wondered if there is a difference between Holy Spirit and Holy Ghost. They are exactly the same thing. They both refer to the breath, to its animating power, and to the soul.

Dove, fire, oil, wind, and water are the symbols of the Holy Spirit. Matthew 3:16, Mark 1:10, Luke 3:22, and John 1:32–33 describe the baptism of Jesus; and the dove is a major part of the event. John 1:32–33 states, "Then John the Baptist gave this testimony: I saw the Spirit come down from heaven as a Dove and remain on Him. And I myself did not know Him, but the one who sent me to baptize with water told me, 'The man on whom you see the Spirit come down and remain is the one who will baptize with the Holy Spirit.'"

When do we receive the Holy Spirit into our lives? The New Testament teaches that we receive the Holy Spirit immediately upon believing in Christ as Savior. All believers in Jesus instantaneously receive the Holy Spirit.

CHAPTER 9

Forgiveness and Humility

The ability to forgive others and the characteristic of humility are true signs of maturity. It takes a mature person to be able to think *outside of oneself* and consider the welfare of others. To forgive and be humble, a person must outgrow the "me first" instinct. When we are small children, we have to have our own way and don't have as much consideration for others. Part of the maturation process is to consider the feelings and well-being of others. We need to learn to think from another person's point of view, not only from our own position. I included the two topics, forgiveness and humility, together in this chapter because they are so closely related. It takes a humble person to have the ability to forgive others when he or she has been wrongfully offended.

As we grow older, hopefully, we learn the reality that forgiveness is actually more beneficial for the forgiver than the person being forgiven. This is a difficult concept to grasp, and some people never do come to the realization that forgiveness makes the forgiver much more at peace. Many people feel a sense of power in hanging onto a grudge against another person. People sometimes think they are hurting the offender by staying mad at him or her. There is a popular phrase that says, "Someone is cutting off their nose to spite their face," which means a person does something that they think will hurt someone without realizing or caring that it will hurt themselves as well. This axiom holds true very often as people believe there is power in their anger, and they are unwilling to let go of this form of control.

Holding a grudge against someone creates stress in the life of the person who was offended. Stress can be very harmful to people, even to the point of causing illness. In addition, it is not healthy to carry anger and bitterness as we go about our daily lives. It can be said that not forgiving someone hurts the offended person more than the offender.

Tied to the idea that it is not healthy to hold anger and conflict in our daily lives is the concept that we must be very prudent in choosing the battles we want to fight in our lives. What issues do we want to let affect our lives, even our daily lives? There can be many issues in a day that require our energy and attention. We must not let situations or circumstances that are not all that important affect us in a negative way. There is so much opportunity to become entangled in conflict on a regular basis in our lives. If we are not careful, we can let conflict and chaos dominate our lives.

We have to guard our peace and be wise in choosing what issues we want to invest energy in. We have only so much time and energy available to us, and we must use our resources wisely. It is beneficial to ask ourselves, *Do I want to become engaged in this particular issue and use up my time and energy? Is this issue worthy of taking away some of my peace?* It is wise to be very careful in determining what issues we choose to take on. As the saying goes, "Choose your battles."

Forgiving people when we are wronged is such a freeing feeling. It is like unloading a burden we have been carrying. Forgiving can give us a feeling of well-being knowing the act of forgiveness is very pleasing to the Lord. Much of Jesus's ministry when here on earth was based on forgiveness. We learn that not only does forgiving make us feel good but that it keeps the door open to reconciliation with the offender.

I think of forgiveness as a three-link chain. One, God has forgiven us for our sins through the death of His Son, Jesus. Second, because of God's merciful forgiveness of our sins, we are expected to forgive others of their sins against us. The Lord's Prayer includes, "Forgive us our trespasses as we forgive those who trespass against us." Finally, the third link of the chain may be the most difficult. We have to learn to forgive ourselves. It is not healthy, and God does not want us to carry the burden of guilt throughout our life. We must confess to the Lord that we are sorry for our wrongdoing, and He will take care of it from there. If we confess our sins, we need not worry about them again.

A crucial mistake I have noticed many people suffer from is *burning bridges*. I have learned we should keep relationships with others open, rather than sever the relationship through actions that end the communication line forever. One never knows when a person can benefit from the help of someone with whom a former conflict existed. I have observed time and again people who were too proud to forgive someone who could have greatly helped the grudge holder in the future.

I have experienced many situations in my life that I was very happy former conflicts were resolved by working the situation out and keeping communication lines open. We never know when we may need assistance in our lives from people we thought our interactions with were complete. Circumstances change in life, and we need as many allies as we can possibly have. Although forgiving to benefit us may sound a bit self-serving, it is always good to repair relationships with others. There may be a lot of goodness in store for both parties involved after forgiveness is granted. God can and will grant blessings for following his instruction to forgive others.

Humility can be defined as follows: a modest or low view of one's own importance. Being humble does not mean a person possessing the quality of humility can't have healthy self-esteem and self-image. On the contrary, humble people commonly are secure in themselves and know their value. They don't have to prove their worth to others. A humble person can accurately and confidently believe that others see them as a person of great worth. The humble person has a way of not exulting him or herself, especially in the presence of others.

I have learned in my interactions with people throughout my life that humility is a very attractive quality. Think of people you know, people who might be considered arrogant or overly proud, and people who demonstrate humility. I would be willing to bet it is easier for you to enjoy the company of humble people compared with arrogant people. Humble people do not fall into a trap that many immature people tend to get caught in. That trap is making excuses for mistakes they make. Some people have trouble owning up to errors or wrongdoings they commit and try to cover for their mistakes by making excuses or blaming the failure on someone else. A humble person usually has the maturity to be accountable for their actions.

Humble people often seem to have a gentle spirit and are easy to be around. They often are good listeners and are genuinely interested in you. Humble people many times have the ability to *draw you out* in conversation, encouraging you to share what is going on in your life.

Arrogant or prideful people can wear you out by centering most of the conversation around themselves. It is sometimes hard to get a word in edgewise when conversing with an overly proud or arrogant person. An arrogant person sometimes appears unable to realize their domination of the conversation.

There are many references in the Bible describing God's disdain for arrogance and love for humility. Proverbs 11:2 says, "When pride comes, then comes disgrace, but with humility comes wisdom." Many people translate the verse to say, "Pride comes before the fall." Seven chapters later, Proverbs 18:12 states, "Before a downfall the heart is haughty, but humility comes before honor." These are only two passages that address God's position comparing humility and arrogance. God's view of the two contrasting traits is a common theme throughout the Bible. James 4:6 summarizes God's attitude about humility and arrogance saying, "God opposes the proud but gives grace to the humble."

I think it is fair to say that all of us need to be on guard against the tendency to be arrogant at times. In our quest to make a good impression in society, we often feel we have to advocate for ourselves. We have to be careful not to self-promote inappropriately. It is very tempting to make ourselves look good, sometimes at the expense of others. We must always keep the feelings and welfare of others in mind. Striving to be humble is pleasing to God's eyes.

I have noticed three common tendencies among people society may consider arrogant or overly proud. One is an inability or reluctance to admit mistakes they may have made. It is as if acknowledging a mistake they made would make them look ignorant or vulnerable. They may have an attitude, consciously or subconsciously, that they are above being wrong.

Another thing which an overly proud person may be reluctant to do is to apologize. The failure to apologize relates directly to the trait mentioned in the previous paragraph, avoiding admitting mistakes. After all, there usually isn't a reason to apologize if a person is never wrong. Reluctance to apologize may be due to feeling vulnerable and having that moment of perceived weakness during the process of apologizing. Quite contrarily, the ability to admit mistakes and apologize is a sign of strong character. As the saying goes, "It takes a big person to admit he or she is wrong." Sometimes when the assignment of fault is up in the air, we need to be the bigger person and admit our wrongdoing in the situation to facilitate the healing process.

The third issue I have noticed people battling pride deal with is an inability to recognize areas of weakness in their lives. It is a real gift to be able to look at ourselves in an objective fashion and assess both our weaknesses and strengths. It takes humility to accurately evaluate ourselves. If we have too much pride, it can be a very difficult task to be totally honest with ourselves. It is crucial to admit and identify our shortcomings so that we can strive to be a better person and better Christian throughout our entire lives. Ironically, by knowing our weaknesses, we can be a stronger person. Accurately identifying our strengths and weaknesses in our lives at an early age also helps choose an enjoyable and rewarding vocation to pursue.

CHAPTER 10

Taming the Tongue

One of the most important life skills we can learn at an early age is the ability to control our tongue. I would bet almost every adult can think back to times when they said things to people they wish they could take back. I'm also sure that most teenagers have also already spoken in their young lives words they regret. Many times, the things said are when the speaker is angry. Other times, the speaker spoke without taking the time to think before revealing words that turned out to be hurtful to someone. One thing we all learn the hard way is that "Once it is out, you can't put the toothpaste back into the tube." Once something is spoken, it can never truly be taken back. Unfortunately, sometimes the hurt caused by damaging words can severely damage or even end relationships. For teenagers, it may be damaging to the relationship of a friendship, a budding romance, with a parent, or with other respected adults.

So when our tongue gets us in trouble, what can we do for damage control? We can apologize, and we can say that we didn't mean it. These things may help, but usually, the damage is already done. Perhaps we didn't entirely mean what we said, but the Bible provides evidence that what we said was in our hearts. Matthew 12:34 includes, "For the mouth speaks what the heart is full of." We tend to speak what is in our hearts.

We must use self-discipline when speaking and consider what we are about to say and how our words might be interpreted. That extra second of consideration may save a lot of pain. Our natural tendency is to speak the first thing we think of, concerning the present conversation. Most of us need to work on being a better listener. As the saying goes, "The Lord gave us two ears and only one mouth for a reason." If you are like me, you sometimes fall into the trap of thinking about what you are going to say next when engaged in a conversation instead of focusing on what the speaker is saying.

Choosing our words wisely is a very valuable tool. Our words can badly injure people if we are not careful. A profound quote says, "The tongue has no bones but is strong enough to break a heart." Another clever and true saying reads as follows, "A broken bone can heal, but the wound a word opens can fester forever." Our words have consequences in our lives.

Taming our tongues can be greatly assisted by help from the Lord. Through the enabling of the Holy Spirit, we can learn to control our tongues. We simply need to pray to the Lord for help in the way we speak. He is willing and able to help us with the issue of our speech. The way we use our words becomes a pattern of living. The way we speak, in large part, reveals our character.

My high school golf coach would say, "You learn a lot about someone by playing a round of golf with them." I have found this statement to be very true as I have gone through life. Much of what you learn about your playing partner is gleaned from what they say and how they act on the golf course. However, it is not only in playing golf with someone that you learn about one's character. Spending time doing anything with someone we recently met teaches us a lot about them, much of it based on the words they use.

It is helpful for us to practice the way we speak. When we use our words inappropriately, we should catch ourselves and recognize our errors. Even if only for a split second, it is good to acknowledge the speaking error. Hopefully, the next time we are about to use similar words, we will be less likely to misspeak and be more likely to use appropriate words. Practicing the way we speak is a lifelong process. Even at this stage of my life, I am constantly working on using better words and a speech pattern more pleasing to God.

When I think back to my junior high and high school years, the issue of taming the tongue comes into full view. Peer pressure has affected the way teenagers speak for generations. In striving for acceptance, we speak the way our peers expect us to talk. Sometimes to impress friends, a teen will use speech that will "blow out the candles of others in order to make their candle glow brighter." It is a sign of maturity to be aware of and sensitive to the feelings of others. Teenagers aren't always aware of the feelings of others and will often say things to draw the laughter of peers at the expense of another person. As mentioned earlier, we need to think from another person's point of view.

It is a difficult task for teenagers to speak properly and avoid inappropriate words. In our society today, we are bombarded with unwholesome language and ungodly inferences through advertisements in the media as well as social media. Also, the content on movies and television shows seems to have almost no boundaries in today's world. Society seems to be trying to tell teenagers that it is okay to talk in an unacceptable fashion. The language on a lot of programming is foul and would have never been permitted in my teenage years, and that is not to mention the sexual content exhibited on television and other mediums. Even advertisements contain unwholesome language and adult themes.

Therefore, inappropriate content is very difficult for teenagers to avoid. Unsuitable language is all around teenagers in today's society. Teenager's inevitable exposure to inappropriate language makes it very difficult to learn to speak in a positive, acceptable fashion. It is crucial for children to be grounded in a strong relationship with the Lord in order to properly process the subject matter they are exposed to in our world today.

Our challenge is to use the tongue in a positive way, one that glorifies God. Growing with gentleness of tongue is a difficult but potentially rewarding life skill. Proverbs 25:15 tells us, "Through patience a ruler can be persuaded, and a gentle tongue can break a bone." There is unlimited benefit to learning to speak in a gentle, controlled manner. Proper speech can help make a great first impression when meeting people. Job interviews put someone who speaks properly at a huge advantage and can be the difference maker between two candidates.

There is immense power in our tongue. We are commanded to wield this power wisely. God desires for us to use our tongue to bring Him glory and to edify others. The word *edify* means to build up another person. Our words can help people feel better about themselves and can even have a healing quality.

Interestingly, two of the Ten Commandments speak about sins of the tongue. One of the commandments tells us not to use the Lord's name in vain. Another of the Ten Commandments directs us against bearing false witness (lying) against someone else. Additional sins of the tongue include the following: boasting, being critical, double-tongued (two-faced), uncontrolled angry words, and hateful speech.

The Bible is very clear in telling us how important our words are to God. Matthew 12:36–37 states, "But I tell you that everyone will have to give account on the day of judgment for every empty word they have spoken. For by your words you will be acquitted, and by your words you will be condemned."

It is evident that taming the tongue is one of the most important things we can learn. It will help prevent us from *burning bridges* in our lives. Controlling our tongues helps keep communication lines open with the people we interact with throughout our lives. I have learned the hard way on more than one occasion how damaging words can be.

Teenagers can avoid a great deal of pain in their lives if they learn to slow down and think an extra split second before speaking. When anger rages inside you, it is wise to be quiet until composure is regained. It is a sign of maturity when we realize that we don't always have to have the last word in a disagreement. That last word often turns out to be words we regret. It is often wise to disengage from a dispute when the temperature gets hot. Most importantly, be aware of the hurt you can cause others by angry and/or critical words.

CHAPTER 11

Handling Conflict

Another important skill a person can develop is the ability to effectively deal with situations where conflict exists. It is certain that we will have conflict with other people throughout our lives, and conflict is especially going to be present in the teenage years. Teens being in school with other children is a hotbed for disagreement and conflict to develop. Teenagers are still maturing and figuring out how to resolve issues and how to compromise. The fact that conflict resolution skills are usually not fully developed in teenagers can lead to some ugly outcomes when teenagers attempt to resolve disagreements with each other.

One of the roadblocks for teenagers to overcome in solving conflicts is the "me first" mentality. Many times in a young person's life, they are accustomed to getting what they want. Sometimes when things don't go a young person's way, anger, frustration, and confrontation are the result. Another reason conflict can develop is the inability to see from another person's point of view. These two problem sources are closely related and have to be developed as the person matures and becomes more experienced with encountering conflict.

Fortunately, there are some skills that can be developed to help the maturation process along and help with resolving conflict. Most of the skills relate to listening, speaking respectfully, being open to and respecting the opinion of others, and taking responsibility for your part of the blame in the disagreement. These skills go a long way in communicating effectively, which is the cornerstone of resolving conflict.

James 1:19 is a wonderful scripture revealing simple but profound advice in avoiding and de-escalating conflict. The passage instructs us, "My dear brothers and sisters, take note of this: Everyone should be quick to listen, slow to speak and slow to become angry."

The scripture indicates the importance of listening. There may be no more important trait to possess than being a good listener. Being a good listener helps you in all areas of your life and will almost certainly increase your friendship circle. If you think about your best friend, chances are they are a good listener.

Being a good listener is especially important in resolving conflict. Many times, conflict starts or continues because multiple parties are talking over each other. When we are talking, we are not listening well, and the resolution process never gets off the ground. A mistake that I've made when arguing is thinking of what I am going to say next, instead of focusing on what the speaker is saying. It is easy to see how a communication barrier can take place under that circumstance.

Another advantage of listening well when in an argument is that it can disarm the person with whom you have conflict. Making eye contact with the speaker and letting them know you are following what they are saying by nodding subtly and demonstrating positive body language can de-escalate the situation. The speaker will usually take your cue and listen to your side of the discussion more objectively. The word *de-escalate* can be defined as reducing the intensity of a conflict or potentially violent situation.

De-escalating the situation is one of the most important things in resolving a heated conflict. Very little can be settled when anger is present. As James 1:19 indicates, be slow to become angry. The passage also tells us to be slow to speak. We should measure our words carefully before releasing them when in a conflict situation.

To be an effective conflict solver, we need to be accountable for our part in the conflict. Usually, there is some fault on the part of both parties involved in the dispute. It is not often that fault is totally on only one person in the conflict. We need to own up and admit to our part of the responsibility for the conflict. We need to avoid making excuses and/or blaming others for what we are responsible for.

Another important skill to learn is the ability to compromise. In resolving conflicts, we can't expect the settlement to go completely in our favor. Compromise is something we will be doing to some degree throughout our lives. It is not only in resolving conflicts where we will be compromising in life but in other situations where negotiations are helpful in coming to a decision.

Not all conflicts end with all parties being happy. Conflict resolution and compromise is a give-and-take proposition. We will win on some issues of the conflict but will be denied what we want in other areas of the dispute. We don't always come to an agreement on all facets of the conflict. As the saying goes, "Sometimes we have to agree to disagree."

I remember being a grade school kid and, on more than one occurrence, complaining to my mother about someone with whom I was having conflict. I would be telling her how unfairly I was being untreated by the person and how all the fault belonged to them. Mother would say to me, "Kill them with kindness." She told me to go out of my way to be extra nice to the person, and then the problem will go away. I found my mother's idea to be very helpful. In many cases, the conflict would de-escalate.

The strategy of being kind to one's adversary is also biblical. Proverbs 25:21–22 says, "If your enemy is hungry, give him food to eat; if he is thirsty, give him water to drink. In doing this, you will heap burning coals on his head, and the Lord will reward you."

By treating your conflict opponent with kindness and respect, the person likely will have difficulty being adversarial with you. They will see goodness in you, even in the wake of the conflict. Best of all, Proverbs 25:22 tells us that the Lord will reward us for treating our enemy with kindness.

Praying for our adversaries is a very powerful tool. Prayer for our conflict opponent has the capacity to soften the hearts of all involved in the conflict and give peace to the prayer petitioner.

Conflicts with friends are a normal part of human relationships. We are going to have plenty of conflict with others in our lives.

Conflict can be resolved in a healthy and constructive manner with effective communication, active listening, and seeing from another's point of view. Honesty and clear communication are vital in total resolution of conflicts.

CHAPTER 12

The Impact of a Compliment and Expressing Gratitude

Just as the tongue can be used to tear people down, it can also be utilized in building people up. In my opinion, complimenting others and expressing gratitude are among the two most underutilized people skills available to us. I have found these two skills to be at or near the top of the list of assets I have used in my professional and personal life to my benefit. We don't often realize how giving a compliment or saying thank you helps us until a certain period of time elapses. Many times, I do not learn how compliments and expressing gratitude have benefitted others until days, weeks, or even years have passed. It sometimes takes time for the impact of the positive words on the receiver to get back to the giver. Many times, a third person, maybe a friend or acquaintance, will tell me later how much a compliment or expression of gratitude meant to the receiver of the positive words.

Sometimes we never learn the appreciation that kind words brought forth. However, after many years of working with people, I know in my heart that a compliment goes a long way in making people feel better about his or herself, and even if appreciation is not expressed by the receiver, the gratitude for the compliment is present.

In the same way, the words *thank you* are so powerful and appreciated. I believe the expression of a thank you is one of the most underused phrases among teenagers. It may be because teens feel a bit awkward or vulnerable in some way when expressing gratitude to others. Teens are at an age where appearances are very important. Teenagers may not have the maturity to realize how good a thank you can make a person feel, both the giver and the receiver.

Saying thank you is a skill that should be taught and reinforced from an early age. It is so common to hear parents ask their children, "What do you say?" when the young child is given something. It seems that parents teach their children this etiquette for a few of the formative years, however, the teaching and reinforcement of expressing thank you may diminish once the child gets to be upper elementary and middle school age. Children are on their own more as they get older, and in middle school, it is not always thought of as being "cool" to show good manners and say thank-you.

Regarding giving compliments to people, it seems people are hesitant to take the step in saying something nice to another person, especially a person the compliment giver doesn't know very well. I believe, many times, there is fear that the compliment will be taken the wrong way, especially in today's sensitivity to being politically correct. If a compliment is given to a member of the opposite sex regarding nice clothing, will the kind words be taken as an inappropriate advance? The same concern could be true of mentioning a stylish haircut.

Some people, especially teenagers, maybe a bit shy, which may prevent them from communicating in a direct, one-to-one fashion. The good thing is that the more you offer compliments, the easier it becomes with each opportunity.

Giving a compliment to someone goes a long way in making the day of the giver and the receiver. Receiving a compliment can help the self-image of a person, especially a person who may not be self-confident. The person giving the compliment will get great benefit from the kind words they deliver as well. The compliment giver usually feels a great deal of satisfaction from making someone feel better about him or herself.

I feel increasingly fulfilled with each passing year as I give compliments and say nice things about people. I believe helping others feel good about themselves is a part of maturing. Giving compliments is a positive example of thinking from another person's point of view. To know the compliment will likely be taken in a positive way is a demonstration of thoughtfulness by the giver. I also believe it is the Holy Spirit working in us as we feel more satisfaction in validating others and pleasing the Lord.

For some teenagers, it may feel unnatural to give compliments at first. Giving compliments is a skill that needs to be developed. Again, giving compliments and saying nice things to people become more normal, the more they are exercised. Expressing compliments is a valuable life skill, one that will benefit a person greatly. The magnitude of how compliments can help a person is impossible to measure. It is usually never known the full impact a compliment can have on the receiver as well as the giver of the kind words. The ability to give compliments makes friendships with a wide spectrum of people more likely. There is a kindness the compliment giver demonstrates that is evident to the receiver of the compliment and other people who may witness the act of kindness.

We should all remember how good a genuine compliment has made us feel. Everyone needs that extra boost kind words can provide from time to time. Thinking back to a time when a compliment really lifted us up should serve as excellent motivation to make others feel good by passing along some kind words.

The skills of giving compliments and expressing gratitude, although two different acts, are very closely related. Compliments make the receiver feel good about him or herself while expressing gratitude for something done for a person shows the gesture is appreciated. Think of times when someone expressed gratitude for something you have done for them. I'm certain you would be more likely to do something else for them in the future than if the person failed to acknowledge the act.

Giving compliments to people and expressing gratitude, in addition to benefiting the receiver, will also make your life better. When you build others up by saying things to benefit them, you will find you also make yourself feel good. There is a lot of truth to the saying, "It is better to give than to receive." If that lesson has not already been learned in life, maturation and life experience will teach it.

You will also learn that skills such as complimenting people and expressing gratitude will make you well-liked by others. People who speak in a positive manner and have a positive attitude are usually welcome in any group of people. If you think about people in your life, I'm confident the ones who speak positive words and have a positive thinking attitude are much more pleasant to be around compared to people with negative attitudes and speech patterns.

Another benefit to expressing gratitude to people and complimenting them when appropriate is that people will be much more willing to assist you in time of need. If a person knows you appreciate an act they do for you, they will be more willing to do another favor for you when the need arises. We should always try to keep our relationships with others strong, and we must take our turn to help others in need. This principle can pay many dividends, even after many years of being out of touch with people as the years pass by. As I mentioned earlier in the book, we should avoid *burning bridges* by damaging relationships in our lives. I can guarantee, through life experience, that learning and utilizing the skills of giving compliments and expressing gratitude will make your life better in many respects.

CHAPTER 13

Bestowing Honor on Others

Giving compliments and expressing gratitude to others is a part of honoring others. However, honoring others goes deeper. To honor means to demonstrate high respect or great esteem for someone. By honoring another, you are saying you see great value in them.

The Bible clearly tells us in 1 Peter 2:17 that we are to honor everyone and not just those we feel deserve to be honored. For example, not all of us have been blessed with great parents, but whether or not they are or were good parents, we are instructed by the Ten Commandments to honor them.

In addition, Romans 13:1–7 tells us to honor those in authority. We may not agree with everything they believe or stand for, but we are still to show them honor. When we honor others, we are given favor in our lives. We receive blessings in our lives for pleasing God by honoring others. If we sow honor, we reap God's favor. Finding favor means gaining approval, acceptance, or special benefits or blessings.

In Leviticus 19:32, we are commanded to honor the elderly by saying, "Stand up in the presence of the aged, show respect for the elderly and revere your God. I am the Lord." Older people have the wisdom to share many of life's challenging topics based on their vast array of life experiences.

Our church leaders are also to be honored. First Timothy 5:17 instructs to show honor by stating, "The elders who direct the affairs of the church well are worthy of double honor, especially those whose work is preaching and teaching." By saying double honor, the verse is heavily emphasizing honoring church leaders. Psalm 22:23 directs us to honor the obvious one, the Almighty God. The verse reads, "You who fear the LORD, praise him! All you descendants of Jacob, honor him! Revere him, all you descendants of Israel!"

Not only are we to honor others, but we are to place others before ourselves. Romans 12:10 teaches, "Be devoted to one another above yourselves." Our goal should be to help others be successful. Helping others be successful sometimes takes sacrifice and great humility. By showing others around us that we care about them and that they are important to us, we can be a blessing in their lives.

Supreme mastery of honoring others is when we can be genuinely happy for others' success, even at the expense of us failing to attain a similar goal. It requires extreme maturity and selflessness to celebrate others' achievements when we are striving for the same accomplishment.

Honoring people should be embedded into young people at an early age as possible. The practice of honoring people will yield many benefits throughout a person's lifetime. The more one honors others, the easier it becomes to do. After a time, showing honor becomes a way of life and one that is a desirable practice in the eyes of God.

Along with honoring their parents, young people should respect other leaders in their lives. Teachers, activity leaders, coaches, church youth group directors, and other adults in authority are to be honored. Teenagers encounter many adults in authority in the school setting. Showing honor to people in authority will make the school experience much smoother and in the end, more enjoyable and fulfilling for teenagers.

One trend in society I have noticed among youth is the reluctance to use the title, mister or miss, when addressing an adult in authority. Many teenagers now address those in authority by only using their last name. Instead of saying, "Mr. Anderson," the student often addresses by saying only, "Anderson." This may seem like a small thing, but I believe it underlines a gradual decline in society of showing respect to elders and those in authority. By properly addressing elders and those in authority, we are bestowing honor on them.

We all should be generous with our honor, and we should take delight in making people feel special. A good goal is to set out each day to make someone feel good about him or herself. In doing so, we will feel better about ourselves for serving God. To edify and build up others is what Christians are called to do.

We should try not to miss an opportunity to show honor to others. Talking good behind someone's back is a great way to show honor. If people are talking about someone not present at the conversation site, bringing up the good qualities of the absent person is a good way to show respect. Talking good behind someone's back is very likely to get back to the person in the same way talking bad about someone finds its way back to the subject of the conversation.

Romans 12:10 (ESV) encourages us, "Love one another with brotherly affection. Outdo one another in showing honor." The direction to *outdo one another* demonstrates the importance that showing honor has in the view of the Lord. It makes one wonder what kind of world it would be if we all strived to outdo each other in showing honor.

CHAPTER 14

The Lost Art of Face-to-Face Communication

Whether it is resolving conflict, complimenting, or expressing gratitude, a person needs to be an effective communicator to get the most out of life. *Communication* can be defined as "the imparting or exchanging of information or news." The definition sounds very simple. However, communication can be very complex and easily misunderstood by the receiver. Much of the success and failure during our lifetime depends on our ability to communicate with others. We need to be tactful at times while other times require us to be more direct and to the point. Learning the tone required for communication in certain situations is a valuable tool. We need to get our message across in a constructive fashion throughout our lives.

With the advances in technology, communication has changed in a huge way. Communicating by text and online have become the preferred methods of communication. It is so easy to text or email someone you need to get in touch with. I believe part of the reason communication has evolved to these methods is that it is quick and doesn't inconvenience either the sender or receiver as much as a phone call or personal visit. At times, I find myself guilty of wanting to avoid uncomfortable small talk and/or an unpredictable flow of conversation that may be present in a discussion with someone I don't know well. If I am communicating with a friend, I am much more willing and comfortable with verbal communication.

There is certainly less face-to-face communication between people today than there was before the advancement in technology over the past decades. We might say that in person, face-to-face communication has become somewhat of a lost art. It seems it has become more difficult and uncomfortable for people to exchange thoughts in person.

The various forms of social media have also been a huge contributor to the breakdown of direct verbal communication. Forums such as Facebook, X (formerly Twitter), and Instagram have definitely had an impact on the decline of verbal communication. A person can often keep up on the happenings of friends and acquaintances through social media without even saying a word to them. Technology is great in many ways in our lives but can hinder in-person, face-to-face communication.

Teenagers are no exception to the modern trend of communication. Generally speaking, teenagers don't speak face-to-face as frequently as in prior generations. Teenagers can often be found in their rooms communicating remotely with friends instead of gathering with friends in person to socialize.

I believe teenagers suffer from a lack of development of their communication skills, which can handicap teens throughout their lives. For example, in job interviews, first impressions are vital. In competing with other applicants, there sometimes isn't much that separates the candidates. Poor communication skills, in many cases, eliminate an applicant right from the start.

Specifics such as making eye contact, a firm handshake, proper attire, posture, and especially verbal and listening skills are extremely important. Demonstrating positive body language is also helpful and important. These presentation qualities are among the components that go a long way in forming a positive first impression. Mastering these skills will be very advantageous in job interviews and life in general.

Being an effective listener is a very valuable communication skill. One underrated listening skill is the ability to *draw out* the speaker. When the speaker finishes a thought, it is effective to ask questions related to what was just spoken. One advantage to drawing out the speaker is you make the person talking feel more comfortable because he or she can sense you are interested in what is being discussed. Also, everyone likes a good listener. Effective listeners can be hard to find. Developing the ability to draw out speakers will serve a person well throughout life.

Another good communication technique is for the listener to clarify what the speaker just stated. This skill is especially useful when the listener is not quite sure he or she is understanding what the speaker is trying to say. This skill is also effective in a conversation where two or more people are disagreeing on a topic. When a person's temper starts to get the best of them, things are often said in the heat of the moment that are spoken without thought. Clarifying what was just said will help the listener confirm what was spoken and may even de-escalate the speaker. An example of a clarifying statement is, "I'm hearing you say that you are against the foreign policy of the president."

One of my favorite communication aids is something modeled to me by the first school principal I worked under. I noticed when he spoke to me and other faculty, he often used our first names in communicating with us. I felt it made his communication more personal, and that he was talking only to me instead of using general lingo he might use to a larger group. The principal's method must have had a positive effect on me because I soon caught myself calling people I was talking with by their first name from time to time in my conversations with them. In my opinion, using people's first names at various times in conversation is a simple way to personalize discussions.

As technology continues to advance, in-person, face-to-face communication skills will likely continue to be more and more of a lost art. Given face-to-face communication has become less common but no less important in society, what can be done to sharpen our in-person communication skills?

Should these life skills and communication skills I've touched on in this chapter be taught in schools? In my opinion, by spending some time on teaching life skills, schools would be setting students up for success in life. There is a significant percentage of children who come from homes that do not make teaching life skills a priority. These children are at a huge disadvantage compared with children who come from homes where skills such as communication skills are taught and reinforced.

If communication life skills were taught from an early age, children and teenagers could present themselves with more confidence and effectiveness. Many of us struggle to remember what we learned in many classes during our school days. Students could take these communication skills with them throughout life and would benefit from them repeatedly.

When I was teaching at the middle school level, we had a teacher/advisee program that taught some life skills and values. I felt the program was very valuable, and I enjoyed teaching the curriculum. It became apparent to me very quickly that students were deficient in many life skill areas.

We actually practiced listening skills such as drawing out the speaker and clarifying statements. After I modeled the desired process to the skills, students would pair up and practice the technique we were working on. We also taught the process of introducing people, avoiding that uncomfortable feeling of two or more people not knowing each other during a conversation or gathering. Other important skills such as eye contact, the importance of a firm handshake, body language, and nonverbal communication were taught and emphasized.

Communication skills need to be taught, emphasized, and corrected at home. Parents have the challenging responsibility to enforce high expectations in the area of proper, respectful communication. It can be a difficult and frustrating job to correct poor communication, but it will likely pay huge dividends in the lives of children.

Proper communication can be practiced at home. Decades ago, great teaching and parenting took place at the dinner table. Parents often demanded that the entire family eat together. It was in the dinner setting that a lot of great communication and parenting took place.

In today's world, schedules are so busy, and kids are in so many around-the-clock activities that it is a big task trying to get everyone at the dinner table at the same time. I believe this trend is detrimental to communication skills and society in general.

It is wise for families to schedule sessions, no matter what time of the day, to talk with each other. Parents can have prepared topics ready for the sessions to supplement conversation. Parents may discover opportunities during these nonconfrontational sessions to gracefully coach communication skills into their children. These types of family sessions would be healthy for families in every way.

It is a great strategy for teenagers to develop excellent in-person, face-to-face communication skills. These skills can give a significant edge in many situations throughout life.

CHAPTER 15

Persistence: The Secret Sauce

As I have progressed through my life, I have come to believe that the trait that highly successful people have that many others don't possess is persistence. We can define persistence as firm or obstinate continuance in a course of action in spite of difficulty or opposition. I love the words, *obstinate continuance* in this definition. A highly successful person is *stubborn* in pursuit of goals. Successful people will not let setbacks stop them from working toward their goals. They continue to strive for goals in spite of roadblocks that will come along. Another word that I like that describes persistence is stick-to-it-iveness. The word stick-to-it-iveness defines itself and is very descriptive.

Most lofty goals we strive to achieve require a lot of time and effort. There will usually be setbacks on the way to attaining lofty goals. This is where persistence separates the successful from the unsuccessful. Successful people have the persistence to determine their own fate in life by digging deep and not letting roadblocks stop them. Persistent people don't like to be *outworked* by anyone. People who turn out less successful in the long run often give up easier than the persistent person when bumps in the road come along. Determination is another word closely linked to persistence. There is no substitution for the characteristic of determination. It is very difficult to derail a determined person on their way to accomplishing a goal. Persistence and determination are real separators regarding success and failure in life.

It is not only in attaining goals that persistence is important but also in persevering through life. Jesus promises there will be adversity in life in John 16:33 when He says, "I have told you these things, so that in me you may have peace. In this world, you will have trouble. But take heart! I have overcome the world." To overcome the trouble this world will bear, persistence and perseverance are required. The words *persistence* and *perseverance* are closely related words. Persistence is a choice while perseverance means surviving the toughest conditions and coming out better on the other side. Both of these qualities are very common in successful people.

We hear the word *potential* so often in life. Potential can be defined as having or showing the capacity to become or develop into something in the future. Unfortunately, many of us fall short of being the best version of ourselves that we can be and maximize the gifts we have.

We hear the phrase *untapped potential* often. It is worth describing what untapped potential is in part because the description helps us understand the word potential better. Untapped potential is the difference between where a person is now and where he or she can be.

How do we tap into our potential? We all have some potential, although some have more natural ability than others, which creates more potential. Our challenge in life is to maximize our potential and utilize our talents to the best of our ability. It is pleasing to God to make the most out of the gifts He has given us.

The reason persistence is the *secret sauce* in determining success is three-fold. One, as I previously mentioned, persistence provides a much greater chance of success in life. It is the separator. Second, persistence is a quality that we can determine whether or not we possess. We don't have to be born with the characteristic of persistence; we can acquire it through self-discipline. Finally, persistence allows us to come as close to reaching our full potential as possible. Maximizing our potential is not an easy thing to accomplish in life. The realization that reaching our potential is difficult is the reason so many people fail to reach their full potential.

To me, one of the greatest compliments a person can give a person is to describe them as an *overachiever*. We can define overachievers as individuals who perform better or achieve more success than was expected. Often, it is through excessive effort and persistence in accomplishing tasks and mastering skills that allows overachievers to accomplish so much. Overachievers seldom get outworked by others in pursuit of their goals.

As an educator and coach, I loved seeing kids I thought of as overachievers come through the system. Some might look at the characterization of an overachiever as a negative label because of the implication that the overachiever has limited abilities and that they don't have as high of a bar to clear.

However, I view maximizing the gifts and abilities we have as fulfilling the destiny God has for us. Very little in life can be more important than fully developing and utilizing the skills God gives us.

On the other hand, observing students and athletes not making the effort to use and develop skills was among the most frustrating situations I encountered as a teacher and a coach. It always seemed such a waste to see a lack of effort in students and athletes *going through the motions* in working toward goals. I remember thinking so many times in my career, *If I could only put person A's natural ability together with person B's work ethic and desire, we would have a superstar.*

The good news is that anyone can have the *secret sauce* of persistence. Some are born with the tenacity to not be stopped from attaining what they desire in life, while others have to develop the characteristic of persistence. It is not easy to develop persistence, but it can be done if it is viewed by someone as important enough to possess. One thing I know from years of observation, persistence is a huge difference maker when it comes to reaching your goals in life. Persistent people are not afraid of starting the process of working toward a goal, while some people procrastinate in beginning the process. In pursuit of accomplishing anything worthwhile, persistent people realize that you don't have to be great to start, but you have to start to be great.

CHAPTER 16

The Book of Proverbs: A "How to Live Your Life" Manual

The book of Proverbs is one of my favorite books of the Bible. Proverbs is a book in the Bible that everyone, especially teenagers should read and reflect upon. It is direct, hard-hitting writing that gets right to the point concerning many practical living topics. The word proverb can be defined as a simple, traditional saying that expresses a perceived truth based on common sense or experience. The book of Proverbs in the Bible is about *wisdom*, and the ability to live life skillfully. God's detailed instruction for His people to negotiate everyday life subjects is provided in Proverbs. Among the topics covered in Proverbs are how to relate to God, parents, authority, peers, neighbors, and teachers. Looking at those topics, it is easy to see how helpful and relevant the book of Proverbs is to teenagers.

The advice given in Proverbs is profound even though a good deal of it is practical. The principal author of Proverbs is Solomon. King Solomon was known as the wisest man who ever lived. He ruled over the kingdom of Israel after the reign of his father, David. Solomon provides a great deal of common sense in Proverbs by using a combination of parables, poetry, short stories, wise expressions, concise questions, and divine perspective helpful in dealing with issues that come up in our lives.

Proverbs often references the words *wisdom, knowledge,* and *understanding.* How do we differentiate between the three closely related words? Scripture points out that understanding comes from learning God's Word. Knowledge comes from the experiences and skills God puts in front of us. Wisdom is the end result if we have used and acquired understanding and knowledge properly. Wisdom could be said to be an accumulation of the understanding and knowledge we receive over time. If we apply the lessons we have learned throughout our lives, we have the opportunity to gain wisdom.

The three traits of understanding, knowledge, and wisdom all come from God. Proverbs 2:6 emphasizes these three gifts from God by saying, "For the Lord gives wisdom; from His mouth come knowledge and understanding."

A great way to illustrate the application of the words *knowledge, wisdom,* and *understanding* is the following sentence: If knowledge is power and wisdom is your choice to use that power, understanding is the execution of your choice to use that power. A situation distinguishing the difference between knowledge and wisdom is the following example. Knowledge is knowing how to use a gun; wisdom is knowing when to use it and when to keep it holstered. One can be knowledgeable without being wise. Maybe this is from which the quote, "A little knowledge is a dangerous thing," was born.

The three words *understanding, knowledge,* and *wisdom* build on each other. Knowledge always comes before wisdom, and to gain understanding, one has to have knowledge and wisdom first and then put them into action.

One very important thing for us to realize is that the key to receiving wisdom is having the humility to accept the words of God. As we discussed in chapter 9, humility is one of the most important traits we can possess. Acknowledging God is the source of everything, and accepting and keeping His words in our hearts requires a humble and meek heart. Everything we have and everything we accomplish is a gift from God. If we are humble, we are always wanting to learn and continuing to seek the best answers.

One of the most profound verses in the Bible is Proverbs 1:7. It says, "The fear of the Lord is the beginning of knowledge, but fools despise wisdom and instruction." The term fear of the Lord relates more to respect and reverence for God than actual fear. To fear God is to know God, and this is where true wisdom can be found. We have to know that God is all-powerful and in control of our lives.

The second part of the verse found in Proverbs 1:7 indicating that fools despise wisdom and instruction, assumes that all lack wisdom by nature, and only those who acquire a fear of the Lord can obtain wisdom. The word *fool* in Proverbs depicts a person who is morally deficient. Proverbs also teaches that we are to submit to God's will in order to gain wisdom.

Proverbs 1:8 is especially important for teenagers to read and absorb. It tells us, "Listen, my son, to your father's instruction and do not forsake your mother's teaching." It is normal for teenagers to have some conflict with their parents as they are being raised. Teenagers and parents are coming from such different perspectives given the difference in age and life experience. Teenagers must realize who is in charge and understand the Bible is clear about obeying parents. Along with the teaching of Proverbs 1:8, the fifth commandment says, "Honor your father and your mother, that your days may be long in the land that the Lord your God is giving you" (Exodus 20:12).

The *Oxford English Dictionary* says *to honor* means "to regard with great respect or high esteem." When honoring our parents, it's essential that we show them respect, accept their authority, obey them, and appreciate them.

Teenagers must resist the temptation to rebel against their parents, even though the teens may believe they are in the right about a particular topic. The Bible commands that we obey our parents, and teenagers should realize that parents are looking out for their best interests.

Along with trying to live a life that pleases the Lord, we obviously want to live life avoiding things He despises. Proverbs 6:16–19 tells us some of the things the Lord frowns on most. This scripture reads, "There are six things the Lord hates, seven that are detestable to Him; haughty eyes, a lying tongue, hands that shed innocent blood, a heart that devises wicked schemes, feet that are quick to rush into evil, a false witness who pours out lies and a person who stirs up conflict in the community."

It would be helpful for all people, young and old, to review Proverbs 6:16–19 periodically. For teenagers, it is very wise to be aware of some of the worst offenses in the Lord's eyes. It is like learning life skills, only the skill here is in avoiding what displeases the Lord. Learning and practicing avoidance of these things God detests at an early age makes it easier to steer clear of committing these grievances throughout life. Avoiding these offenses not only pleases the Lord but will make a person more respected and well-thought-of by others.

For me, Proverbs 22:1 is one of the most important and true verses in the book of Proverbs. The verse reads, "A good name is more desirable than great riches; to be esteemed is better than silver or gold." This scripture speaks to the importance of maintaining a good reputation. If we live a life pleasing to God and live up to our word, we will have a good reputation. At the end of the day, being highly thought of is more important than the assets we acquire.

Earlier in the book, we talked about peer pressure and how powerful it is. It is very important for teenagers to choose good company. Good friends make life so much easier and more rewarding. A positive, supportive peer group makes it easier to do the right things, and chances are that avoiding trouble will more often be attainable. Proverbs 13:20 reinforces choosing good company by saying, "Walk with the wise and become wise, for a companion of fools suffers harm." The company we keep can either make us or break us. People, especially youth, become a product of those we hang out with.

Another great lesson Proverbs teaches us is found in chapter 14:29, which tells us, "Whoever is patient has great understanding, but one who is quick-tempered displays folly." Patience is a wonderful skill, and a person seldom regrets the virtue of taking the time to reflect on the situation at hand before making an important decision. We so often say or do something we later wish we could take back when we speak or act out of anger. We need to learn to *hold our tongue* and think before we react. As we talked about earlier, it is so easy and potentially damaging to *burn bridges* connecting us with other people.

Proverbs is wonderful information to help us to live wisely, the way God wants us to conduct ourselves. It is written in easy-to-understand passages that contain so much common sense. Truly, Proverbs is the book of wisdom.

CHAPTER 17

Hey, Teens, Adults Are Not Your Enemy

It was very fulfilling for me to spend my years as a teacher and coach working with teenagers. In all but six of my thirty-three-year career, my teaching assignment was teaching physical education, along with some health education, at the middle school level, grades 6 through 8. My coaching assignments ranged from working with seventh graders through seniors in high school.

My coaching assignments included fifteen years as Head Boys Basketball Coach, nineteen summers as Legion Baseball Coach, and thirty-three years (and counting) as Head or Assistant Boys and Girls Golf Coach. These seasons, especially the basketball and baseball assignments, were intense with a lot of work put in and high expectations to win. The basketball season was not only intense but very long. At the varsity level, the season lasts four months. The seasons working with the high school-aged kids were long enough for me to get to know the kids pretty well. I got to know kids through their elation in times of success and their frustration in disappointing times.

In the last half of my career in education, I coached boys and girls in various sports at the seventh and eighth-grade level including girls' volleyball. In working with kids in extracurricular activities, I had a chance to get to know the students in a different light. I appreciated the experience I received from coaching to go along with my teaching assignment. The different settings, along with a wide range of exposure in age, gave me a well-rounded view of the mindset of a teenager. I also had the opportunity to work with kids from all backgrounds and motivation levels. In teaching middle school physical education, I came to realize quickly that a percentage of the kids did not want to be in school for one reason or another.

One of the things I learned is that a teenager's trust and respect in an adult has to be earned. A teen has to know the adult cares about them and that the adult is not there only to wield power over them. As the saying goes, "Students don't care how much you know until they know how much you care." As a former teacher, I can testify that saying is very true. Many children have had negative experiences regarding authority and interaction with adults.

Because adults are often in positions of authority over teenagers, the teens might view some adults as somewhat of an opponent. If a child hears an answer or gets a result from a teacher contrary to what they want pertaining to a situation, the teenager might start to develop an adversarial view of the adult in power. This view could generalize into a belief that all teachers are out to get students.

Parents often have to make decisions that their children don't want to hear or abide by. Teenagers have to mature and realize that parents have a responsibility to keep their children safe and protect their best interests. Many times, parents have to make unpopular calls, going against the desires of their children.

When parents go against the wishes of their children, they are often making a decision to safely guide teenagers through situations that can have negative results. These decisions are made out of love and from life experiences adults have already gone through. Teenagers sometimes think their parents are out to make the teen's life miserable by keeping them from doing fun things. This assumption is usually the farthest thing from the truth.

One of the most famous Bible verses about parenting is found in Proverbs 22:6. The NIV Bible states, "Start children off on the way they should go, and even when they are old they will not depart from it." Other versions of the Bible start the verse with, "Train up a child in the way he should go."

Teenagers must understand that training their children is what parents are directed to do according to the Bible. Holding teens accountable and keeping them out of harm's way is not only biblical, but it is in the best interest of the child. Over the long term, teenagers will realize the motives of the parents were sound and wise.

Children coming to find out years later that their parents were not so ignorant after all, reminds me of a quote credited to Mark Twain. The quote goes like this: "When I was a boy of 14, my father was so ignorant I could hardly stand to have the old man around. But when I got to be 21, I was astonished at how much the old man had learned in seven years."

I think many adults can fully identify with the Mark Twain quote. Parents' advice seems so constrictive or out of date as we are growing up. As time passes, many times, we realize that our parents were right all along and probably saved us from physical and/or emotional harm in our vulnerable years. Adults often admit that they end up raising their own children with similar rules, philosophies, and guidelines as the adult's parents imposed on them.

We should learn as we age that there is no substitute for life experience. Life experience is a great teacher. Wise teenagers learn to acquire wisdom from the example of their parents and other trusted adults, and not to always contradict instruction from parents and teachers. By learning from their parents' experiences in life, teenagers can avoid making some of the same mistakes their parents made when they were in their teens. Preventing their teenagers from making harmful, sometimes devastating, choices, is why parents are so firm in their stances regarding certain situations. Your parents already know how the situation will likely turn out before it even happens. As the saying goes, parents have already "been there and done that."

In writing this book, I felt the need to include this chapter because I learned in my teaching and coaching career that a number of teenagers didn't take full advantage of the resources parents, teachers, activity advisors, coaches, and other trusted adults provided for them. I believe for some teenagers, it is the perception projected by their peers that contributes to the lack of fully using the help teachers, coaches, and advisors could afford them. This relates back to the peer pressure teens face discussed earlier in this book.

In some peer groups, it is not viewed as "cool" to interact with teachers in a positive way. To put a humorous spin on it, it is like *fraternizing with the enemy*. Teachers represent authority, and some teenagers have trouble accepting and submitting to authority. Some peer groups in school have an *us versus them* attitude regarding coexisting with teachers in a school setting. This view is unfortunate because most of the adults who serve as potential resources to kids are just waiting to be of assistance to children. Most educators entered the teaching and coaching profession to help kids. Along with teachers and administrators, schools usually have a great staff that loves to help kids. School paraprofessionals, secretaries, counselors, cooks, and custodians help countless students with their school experience.

As I reflect on my career as a teacher and a coach, I have come to realize that one of the major differences between successful students and athletes and ones who fall short of expectations is the willingness to accept help from adult resources available to them. Parents, teachers, coaches, advisors, youth group leaders, and other trusted adults can offer knowledge, experience, and instructional skills to make the teenage years more fruitful, productive, safe, and growth-filled.

Most successful students and extracurricular participants have learned to use adult resources to their advantage to help them get on the path they want to be on as they complete the first one-fourth of life. Wise teenagers learn not to *burn bridges* and use adults as vehicles to success.

CHAPTER 18

Establish an Early Relationship with God

There are so many advantages to developing a relationship with God at as early of an age as possible. No age is too young to remember and recruit the favor and protection of God through reverence to Him. God can and will give you the strength and wisdom to do the right thing in difficult situations. In general, teenagers know right from wrong but often need reinforcement to resist temptation and do the right thing. With God, you have a majority, no matter how many people you may be differing with. If you have developed a relationship with Him, He will give you the wisdom and resolve to handle the situation properly.

Here are some reasons to establish a relationship with God as early as possible. These reasons will be of great benefit in all areas of life, including dealing with peer pressure. Concerning peer pressure and peer approval, a relationship with God yields many benefits.

True friends will always accept you for who you are. The sheer number of friends may be important to some teens. However, as the years go by the number of friends, you have may become less important. At the same time as maturity takes place, people begin to realize that the quality of the friendship is what really matters. We are truly blessed if we have one true friend in our lifetime. If we have two or three close, sincere, and trusted friends, we are abundantly blessed.

I'm not talking about casual friends, I'm referring to intimate friends with whom you can share anything, without concern of the information ever coming back to harm you. These types of friends care about your welfare as much as they care about their own. The motives of this type of friend are as pure as the driven snow when it comes to their dealings with you. Their support and counsel are invaluable. Friends like these are extremely hard to find.

It is comforting to know that we all have a friend who is even better than the best friend we could ever have on this earth. This friend is Jesus Christ who died on the cross for forgiveness of our sins. Hebrews 13:5 says in part, "He Himself has said, I will never leave you nor forsake you." Because Jesus is always with us, we can get through anything this life can throw at us. Jesus will always be there for us even when we are not there for Him. Issues such as peer pressure will not be so intense when we remember that Jesus is in our corner. The apostle Paul says in Romans 8:31, "If God is for us, who can be against us?"

In addition to the help of Jesus in dealing with peer pressure and peer approval, we can also look at some practical points to put the need for the acceptance of our peers in perspective. A teenager's network of friends changes quickly over their next decade of life. Therefore, there is no reason a teenager shouldn't take the risk of upsetting a peer through contradiction and standing up for what one believes. Friendship circles will change as teens move from middle school to high school and from year to year and even within a school year as class schedules change.

Then after high school graduation, friendship groupings often change drastically as students go their separate ways. After postsecondary education and other endeavors after high school, a new group of friends likely starts again as young adults enter the workforce.

The point is that even one year can seem like an eternity to a teenager. It seems to them that the friends they have in school are the same ones they will have throughout their lives. Nothing could be farther from the truth. When people get to their midtwenties and beyond in age, many school friends will be only a distant memory. It is difficult for a teenager to comprehend how friendship circles will change rapidly in life, particularly in the first quarter of life.

Decisions made when under peer pressure must be based on what is best for the individual and what he or she believes in. The decisions shouldn't be made as a result of FOPO (fear of other people's opinions). Values and beliefs should not be compromised as a result of peer pressure. True friends will support your decisions and respect you for standing up for your beliefs. When dealing with peer pressure and peer approval situations, it is extremely advantageous to have a relationship with God. He will direct your steps, giving you wisdom and courage to do the right thing. Psalm 37:23–24 says, "The Lord makes firm the steps of the one who delights in Him; though he may stumble, he will not fall, for the Lord upholds him with His hand." We must always remember He is the friend who will never leave us or forsake us, and He is ultimately the only one who matters.

Another advantage to having a relationship with God at an early age is that a person has more years to worship Him. The more someone glorifies the Lord, the stronger the two-way relationship becomes. An early relationship with God also enables one to have more time to get to know the Lord better by studying His word. Of course, one of the most effective ways of getting into God's word is through reading and reflecting on Bible scripture. Some people choose to read the Bible cover to cover often starting with the New Testament. Another way to read the Bible is to pick out books of the Bible to read in an order chosen by the reader. In addition, there are many wonderful sermons and messages by preachers available at churches, online, and on television.

Today's youth are at a huge advantage due to advances in technology and teenagers' keen knowledge of how to use technology. The internet can be very ungodly if used the wrong way. It can be a weapon of Satan if used for the wrong purpose. Exposure to pornography is one very negative aspect of the internet. Also, the internet can be a source of cyberbullying, which has become a huge problem for teenagers who are targets of this type of harassment. However, I have found the ability to Google Bible scripture to be extremely beneficial to me. The internet can get a person quickly to the correct Bible chapter and verse. The internet will also explain the meaning of the scripture and explain in what context the passage was used. I have found researching scripture to be very easy, interesting, insightful, and time-efficient.

Reverent worship of the Lord, studying His word, and spending time with Him through prayer lead to God's favor and blessing in one's life. Favor and blessings are extremely wonderful and beneficial in any person's life, especially teenagers as they go through formative years of life. To put it simply, by having a relationship with God, you have the creator of the universe as your advocate. The Lord will be with you as you negotiate the adversity life brings. An advocate is a person who represents another person's interests. Can you think of a more powerful advocate? A relationship with God has Him at the ready to help you in big or small situations. It is not a coincidence that things often break in favor of a person who has a relationship with God.

Developing a strong, early bond with God will bring about both explosive blessings and subtle blessings. Explosive blessings are powerful, sometimes life-changing, blessings that occur. A much sought-after college scholarship or meeting a potential soulmate for marriage would be examples of explosive blessings. Subtle blessings are less significant, but nonetheless, very helpful blessings, which might be bestowed throughout the day. A teacher giving a student extra help in understanding a lesson, or a classmate offering to sit with a student during lunch after seeing the student is having a bad day at school are examples of subtle blessings.

The Lord will take care of you, especially if you have developed a relationship with Him. The bond with Him must be a two-way street in order to be a true relationship. God will always be there for you, but in order to experience His complete blessings for you, the relationship must be nurtured through prayer, worship, and obedience. Many times, God will advocate for you even without your awareness. His favor will cause things to break in your favor. In fact, others may even notice your fortune and call you lucky. God's favor is no coincidence, and He is well able to provide blessings and protection for you.

An early relationship with the Lord will grant protection from not only the enemy (Satan) but also the many challenges in society. Middle school and high school can be difficult years for teenagers. Cliques have always been a potential problem for kids at schools. A clique may be described as an exclusive group of people who share common interests and beliefs. Children can be very cruel to one another through exclusion, sometimes having rigid criteria for acceptance into a peer group.

Bullying is another timeless evil that has always existed in schools. In recent times, there has been a nationwide awareness concerning bullying. There are more methods of bullying, in large part because of social media, available in today's society compared to the predominantly physical intimidation of yesteryear.

One of the most common forms of bullying in today's world is cyberbullying, using the internet as a weapon to inflict psychological harm. Social media provides an easy and sometimes vicious way to attack victims without even being face-to-face. Experts contend that cyberbullying is the cause of many teenage suicides. It is now more important than ever for teenagers to have the protection of the Lord as they go through middle school, high school, and the first years following high school.

There are countless reasons that it is a tremendous advantage for young people to have a strong relationship with God. Ecclesiastes 12:1 reveals, "Remember your Creator in the days of your youth, before the days of trouble come and the years approach when you will say, 'I find no pleasure in them.'" For young people, a relationship with God can be such a rock of stability and guiding light as they go through the vulnerable years of youth. The assistance of God is invaluable as young people fully develop their value system and identity.

When it comes right down to it, establishing a relationship with God is what putting on God's armor is all about. We must take the time and make the effort to get to know God's word, worship and communicate with Him in prayer, and attempt to live a life that will greatly please Him. If we live our lives in that manner, the parts of God's armor will automatically fasten to us. We will have the protection we need, not only for spiritual warfare but for all areas of our lives. We will have a best friend who will advocate for us in times of need and give us favor, providing an advantage in getting us to what He has destined for our lives. Let's make life easier, more rewarding, and more fruitful by putting on the armor of God.

EPILOGUE

Bringing It All Together

When I retired from teaching in 2012, I thought that I had it made from that point on. I believed life would be easy and fulfilling as I lived out the rest of my life. I would be able to do whatever I wanted, and I would have far fewer obligations than before. At first, things were great. I was so happy not to have to wake up by an alarm clock early each morning, and that I could sleep in as late as I wanted.

However, as time passed by, I noticed that I lost my sense of purpose in life. It felt unusual to me that days could pass by, and nobody would remember that John Gloege even existed. The days passed by at my former school just fine without me.

By retiring, I had removed my vehicle, in a large way, to serve others. I started to exist through life day after day without being needed by anyone. I began to become a *homebody* and wanted to avoid social interaction.

You may wonder why I am writing about my retirement and how it made me feel. The reason is that we all need a purpose to bolster our self-esteem. No matter what age we are, we have a desire to be needed.

For me, this sense of lack of purpose caused by retirement has been filled by writing. I have been called by the Lord to write two books, the first being *Your Reward Shall Not Come of This Earth*. The joy and benefit of writing these books have been three-fold. First, the books I have written are my attempt to serve the Lord and spread His

Word. Second, writing has filled the sense of purpose void I developed since retirement. Finally, writing the two books has brought me closer to realizing my potential to live out God's full destiny for my life.

Although I've always enjoyed writing, being an author was not in the forefront of my retirement plans. I thought my work was done. However, my writing has shown me that we all must keep an open mind to what God has in store for us at any age. Keeping an open mind and exploring new things is especially important during the teenage years. Even in being a teenager, it is important to have a sense of purpose. We have to feel like we matter and that we are a link in the chain of the functioning of something.

Teens may be at the point where they are wondering where they fit in the grand scheme of life. Do not fear, your purpose will be revealed at some point as you move through your life. If you are struggling to find your purpose, be sure to be vigilant in watching for what God's destiny may be for you.

For teenagers, it is very beneficial to try as many activities as you can. Schools have so many activities available for students to participate in. Just a few of the extracurricular programs available are sports, band, choir, student government, debate, drama club, academic clubs, and art club. In fact, these days there are even opportunities such as video game development club and robotics competitions. There is something for everyone, and teens should be encouraged to try as many different activities as possible to uncover hidden interests and talents. Teens are at such an early part of life that they need exposure to help discover where their talents and interests lie.

Teenagers must resist the temptation to feel like there is something wrong with them if they don't have a firm grasp of what their interests and talents are, and what they might want to pursue for a career. It is very common for teens to be in this uncertain situation. By keeping an open mind, experimenting with different activities, and staying aware of opportunities to explore, teenagers give themselves a much better chance of uncovering interests and vocation possibilities.

To address all of the issues and potential problems that can serve as roadblocks to today's youth, teenagers can give themselves a mile-long head start by enlisting the guidance of the Lord and putting on God's armor. Life is challenging enough with God at one's side. I can't imagine what it would be without Him at your side. Don't wait and think that you will meet up with God later. There is intense spiritual warfare going on in our world today. Every day we fail to enlist the help of God in our lives, the more opportunity for us to be misled. Remember, the full armor of God includes truth, righteousness, the gospel, faith, salvation, the Word of God, and prayer. Also, use the wisdom and life experience of trusted adults as a resource in your lives.

The best thing a teenager, and any adult, can do is recruit God as your best friend. As He says in Romans 8:31, "If God is for us, who can ever be against us?" A close relationship with God comes with an insurance policy. As stated in Hebrews 13:5, the Lord says, "I will never leave you or forsake you." The other part of the insurance policy assures us of inheriting eternal life. God is just waiting for you to request Him to lead you through life.

ABOUT THE AUTHOR

John Gloege graduated from Glenwood High School in Glenwood, Minnesota, in 1974. He was very active in athletics, participating in football, basketball, baseball, golf, and track. John went on to earn his undergraduate degree in physical education, health education, driver education, and coaching at St. Cloud State University in St. Cloud, Minnesota, in 1979. John played college baseball at SCSU for four years. He received his master's degree in Curriculum and Instruction from the University of St. Thomas in 1985. John taught in the Princeton School District in Minnesota for thirty-three years, spending all but six of his years at the middle school level.

He served as Princeton High School Boys head basketball coach for fifteen years, coached American Legion Baseball for nineteen summers, and is still currently serving as assistant boys and girls high school golf coach. After the majority of his coaching was completed, John embarked on a twenty-five-year basketball, football, and volleyball officiating career. John has served in many capacities in the church over the years. Recently, together with his wife, Shirley, he has led Sunday services on a semi-regular basis at Freemont Village, an assisted living / memory-care / independent living facility in Zimmerman, Minnesota.

www.ingramcontent.com/pod-product-compliance
Lightning Source LLC
Chambersburg PA
CBHW022050150726
47990CB00003B/1037